Famous Dave's
Rib-O'Licious!

AWARD-WINNING BARBEQUE
AND GRILLING RECIPES

by "Famous Dave" Anderson,
America's Rib King

www.famousdaveanderson.com

Rib-O'Licious!

The LifeSkills Center for Leadership
Email: info@lifeskills-center.org

Library of Congress Catalog Number:
98-093988
ISBN: 978-0-9668548-2-4

Edited, Designed, and Manufactured by

SOUTHWESTERN
Publishing Group

2451 Atrium Way
Nashville, Tennessee 37214
800.358.0560

Art Direction: Brad Whitfield
Photography: Mike Rutherford
Food Styling: Mary Ann Fowlkes
Recipe Editor: Debbie Van Mol, RD
Production Designer: Gary Moser
Production Director: Mark Sloan
Editorial Director: Mary Cummings
Cook: Dave Anderson

All location photography was shot at
Famous Dave's restaurants.

Manufactured in the
United States of America

First Printing: 1999
Second Printing: 2001
Third Printing: 2004
Fourth Printing: 2012

A portion of the proceeds from the sale of this book are being donated for the betterment of youth, primarily Native Americans.

The LifeSkills Center for Leadership is a nonprofit foundation set up by the David W. Anderson family. The foundation is fortunate to have an opportunity to make a difference by "turning today's challenges into tomorrow's opportunities," through training in leadership, communication, team building, character development, and goal setting.

Foundation accomplishments have provided funding to help build a school roof and to purchase computers, food, and clothing for families in need. It also supports various youth programs, alcohol and drug awareness programs, and treatment services for youth and adults. Long-range goals include building a life-skills training facility where young people will have an opportunity to learn leadership skills that will make a difference within themselves, their families, schools, and communities.

The Anderson family would like to thank you for purchasing this cookbook. We know you will enjoy our award-winning sauces and recipes—at the same time making a difference in the lives of young people. Please visit The LifeSkills Center for Leadership at our website: **www.lifeskills-center.org**

Thanks for helping us make a difference.

Famous Dave

"Famous Dave" Anderson

Foreword

The barbeque community is filled with colorful characters passionate about their chosen sport/art form/culinary technique. After all, barbeque is America's Cuisine. David Anderson is definitely one of the more colorful personalities in our barbeque family. From his Famous Dave's of America eateries to his award-winning sauces and rubs, from his catering to his competition in barbeque contests, Dave is highly visible in the industry.

He is also a highly successful entrepreneur whose whole motivation is to give back to others and the community. He has donated millions to charities, and, with this book, he will further that goal, funding a life-skills camp for disadvantaged youth.

"Famous Dave" Anderson describes himself as "a passionate cook." Dave is a serious student of food and cooking. His study of barbeque has taken him all across America, and he's developed the recipe for dang good barbeque. In the process, he's also experienced all types of regional American cooking—from fine dining to down-home.

Rib-O'Licious! is Famous Dave's tribute to real American food. He's taken the best recipes from local eateries, and perfected them for the home cook. Dave has searched, recreated, and improved them, making these formerly ordinary recipes extraordinary.

This is the ultimate comfort food cookbook. It's food that people love to eat. Dave's outdone himself this time, but as Zig Zigler says in his profile of Dave in *Success for Dummies*, Dave "is just getting started." I hope so.

Carolyn S. Wells, Ph.B.

Executive Director
Kansas City Barbecue Society

*Memphis in May with
Tennessee Governor Don Sundquist
and Nick Vergos of the famous Rendezvous*

"Restaurateur Of The Year"
— Mpls/St. Paul Magazine,
    Minneapolis, MN

"Entrepreneur Of The Year"
of Minnesota & the Dakotas
— Ernst & Young, NASDAQ, USA Today

"1997 Hot Concept"
— Nation's Restaurant News
    names Famous Dave's one of the
    Hottest Concepts in America.

"Hot New Concept"
— Chain Leader
    National Restaurant Chain Publication

"Best New Restaurant"
— Madison Capital Times, Madison, WI
    Mpls/St. Paul Magazine, Minneapolis, MN

"Best Restaurant Design"
Starr Award
— Minnesota Shopping Center Association

"Best Restaurant Promoter"
— Mpls/St. Paul Magazine, Minneapolis, MN

"Best Traditional Take-Out Menu"
— National Barbecue Association

"Greatest Ribs in America"
— Great American Rib Cookoff, Cleveland, OH

"Greatest Sauce in America"
— Great American Rib Cookoff, Cleveland, OH

"Best Sauce"
Critic's Choice
— Twin Cities Ribfest, Minneapolis, MN
People's Choice
— Indianapolis Ribfest, Indianapolis, IN

"Best Barbecue Sauce in America"
Mild Tomato Category
— American Royal Barbecue Contest,
    Kansas City, MO

"Best Ribs" & "Best Sauce"
— Naperville Ribfest, Naperville, IL
    Appleton Post-Crescent, Appleton, WI
    Des Moines Register, Des Moines, IA
    Madison Magazine, Madison, WI
    Mpls/St. Paul Magazine, Twin Cities
    Ribfest, Minneapolis, MN
    Fargo Dome Ribfest, Fargo, ND
    Indianapolis Ribfest, Indianapolis, IN

"Best Desserts"
— Minnesota Monthly, Minneapolis, MN

"Best Pancakes"
Critic's Choice
— Golden Gopher Pancake Cookoff,
    University of Minnesota

"Best Take-Out"
— Mpls/St. Paul Magazine,
    Minneapolis, MN

"Best Last Meal In Minnesota"
— Mpls/St. Paul Magazine,
    Minneapolis, MN

"If Barbeque were a religion
Dave Anderson would be the
Reverend Billy Graham."
— Twin Cities Business Monthly

"...the best good old
All-American fare around."
— Twin Cities Business Monthly

"Attention to detail is
one of (Dave) Anderson's
trademarks."
— Nation's Restaurant News

"...Reminiscent of
American...joints which
dotted the landscape fifty
years ago"
— Where Magazine

"Adam wouldn't have given
up this rib."
— B. Whitfield, BBQ connoisseur

"Famous Dave's
all-American BBQ feast
delivers an embarrassment
of riches"
— Chicago Magazine

"Absolutely the best I've
ever tried"
— Naperville Sun

"You know you're in a
good restaurant when you're
sitting there thinking of people
you have to share it with"
— Appleton Scene

"Famous Dave's does some
pretty mean ribs...intense rib
eating gratification"
— Chicago Sun Times

*Famous Dave's award-winning
national cooking team*

My Thoughts On Cooking

This cookbook does not feature "fast 'n easy recipes" so if you're looking for something to throw together in fifteen minutes—forget it. This is not a diet cookbook. Don't even think of trying to figure out how to make these recipes lowfat. And, if you're looking for trendy, exotic cuisine, look somewhere else. This cookbook is really about passion: my quest for the "best of the best" of foods you already know. Legendary American classics. I have never been satisfied with making something that is just average. I want my cooking to be great cooking. I want people to remember the great meal that I cooked for them. This is my expression of passion.

To me, the most important part of creating food that is tasty, full-flavored, and memorable is relentless attention to details: flavor and texture profiles, plus how good something smells while cooking or being served. Early on when I started fooling around with my first barbeque sauces, I quickly realized I didn't know a thing about seasonings. I wasn't at all familiar with herbs, spices, or natural flavorings. I didn't know what they looked like, how they tasted, or how to use them, much less how to pronounce most of them. And, the more I cook, the more I realize how much I don't know.

Developing my barbeque sauces, I have spent over 25 years trying to figure out what tastes good. I have taken whole mouthfuls of different herbs, spices, fruits, and vegetables just to understand the complex flavor nuances and how they interact with each other. I have tasted them raw, cooked, roasted, grilled, steamed, fried, and microwaved. I'm almost embarrassed to tell people what's been in this mouth! I have sautéed them in regular butter, unsalted butter, canola oil, sunflower oil, and peanut oil, etc., blanched them, and chopped them, coarse-ground them, fine-ground, diced, and minced them. And I've experimented with adding ingredients at various points in the cooking process to see how they react at different cooking temperatures.

I cringe when I see folks just grabbing any ingredient off the shelf when cooking a recipe. Often, I see shoppers in the grocery store wondering which product of the huge variety to buy. The only way to know is to buy them all, taste them all, and keep notes on the taste differences. When developing a recipe which calls for mustard, I will buy every mustard available to discover which has the right flavor profile that will make the recipe I'm working on outstanding. For example, over the years, I have identified the best-tasting Worcestershire sauces, mustards, apricot jams, and so on. Even the same seasoning from another manufacturer will taste different.

Only top-of-the-line ingredients, guaranteed fresh, are acceptable to me—this is non-negotiable. In fact, at home everything gets tossed every six months, and I start all over again. This seems like a lot of work—and it is. But it isn't drudgery if you have a passion for great-tasting food. My goal is to develop recipes that are so outrageously full-flavored that they will slap your taste buds awake! I've done this research so you won't have to, and I've given brand names and sources, both on the recipes and in the Ingredient Preferences (page 158). If I list a particular ingredient, you should make every attempt to try to find that ingredient to make the recipe as close to the product that I so diligently created. If you deviate from my list of ingredients, you will not be achieving exactly the same great taste, although it will still be some of the best food you've ever tasted.

There are no shortcuts to great-tasting food. Preparing food requires patience, practice, passion, exact measuring, attention to details, and a love for cooking. Most of all it takes time: time to find the right ingredients; time to find the freshest ingredients; time to assemble everything necessary to make a recipe; time to measure accurately; time to cook the recipe correctly. And it takes time to dress a table and room appropriately, to provide a cheerful atmosphere and the right music so your family or good friends can share a memorable meal.

And all this business about being "Famous"… I always tell people, "It's the ribs that are famous, and I'm only just the cook!" Just remember that "creativity has no boundaries," and that is the case whether in the kitchen or in front of the smoker—where possibilities are endless.

When I appeared on Food Network's *Best In Smoke* in 2011, I made up my mind that I was going to have fun, and all the folks in barbeque land would appreciate the pigs on my head… it's what we do! As a top three finisher in the barbecue showdown, my goal was to do well in the competition and make the world laugh! I managed to do both and even picked up some life lessons along the way. I was truly honored to be a part of the show.

In this tradition, I feel very honored to be a cook.

Famous Dave

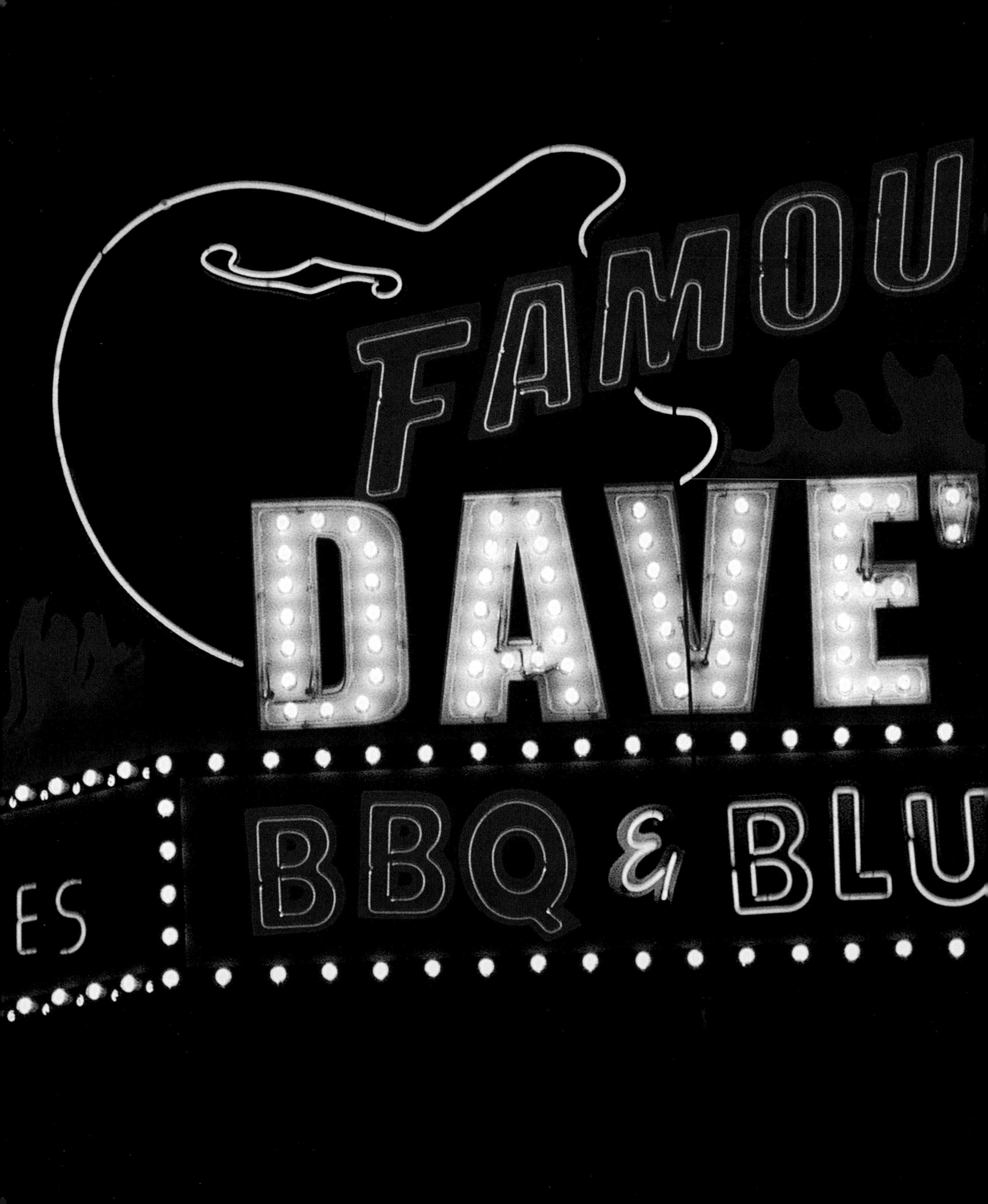
FAMOU
DAVE'
BBQ & BLU
ES

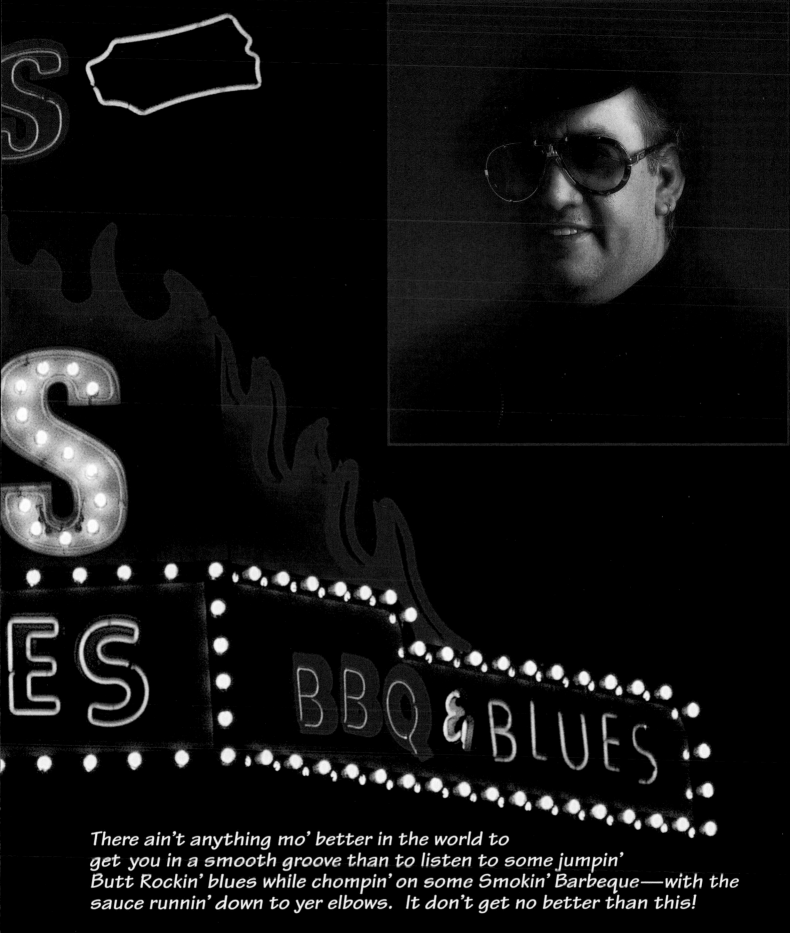

There ain't anything mo' better in the world to
get you in a smooth groove than to listen to some jumpin'
Butt Rockin' blues while chompin' on some Smokin' Barbeque—with the
sauce runnin' down to yer elbows. It don't get no better than this!

9

BLUES JOINTS & STOREFRONTS

BORN IN CHICAGO, I'VE HAD THE OPPORTUNITY TO EXPERIENCE SOME OF THE BEST COOKING IN A TOWN THAT HAS IT ALL. WHETHER YOU LIKE THE FANCY STUFF, ETHNIC FOODS, OR STOREFRONT RESTAURANT FARE, WHERE I REALLY LIKE TO EAT— CHICAGO HAS IT. MY DAD WAS AN ELECTRICIAN WHO OFTEN WORKED ON SOME OF THE BIG BUILDINGS DOWNTOWN. WHEN IT WAS LUNCHTIME, HIS BLACK CO-WORKERS ALWAYS SEEMED TO KNOW WHERE THE BEST BARBEQUE WAS, AND IT WASN'T TOO LONG BEFORE HE WAS BRINGING THESE RIBS HOME IN HIS LUNCH BUCKET. THIS WAS MY FIRST EXPERIENCE WITH REAL BARBEQUE, THE KIND THAT'S BEEN SLO-SMOKED ALL DAY BY SOME STREET CORNER VENDOR, OVER SMOLDERING CHARCOAL AND GREEN HICKORY IN A 55-GALLON DRUM.

ONE OF MY FAMILY'S FAVORITE BARBEQUE RESTAURANTS WAS A PLACE CALLED EDDY'S, LOCATED ON A SIDESTREET ACROSS FROM THE LOGAN STREET "L" STATION. THEY HAD A SMOKER FULL OF SMOKIN' SPARERIBS RIGHT IN THE WINDOW WITH A SIGN THAT BOASTED "WE SELL OVER 7 TONS OF RIBS EVERY MONTH!" YOU KNEW IT HAD TO BE GOOD BECAUSE CHICAGO'S FINEST WOULD OFTEN BE PARKED RIGHT OUT FRONT.

SWEET HOME CHICAGO, THE WINDY CITY, IS THE HOME OF THE BLUES (ALTHOUGH MEMPHIS PROBABLY DISAGREES). CHICAGO HAS ITS OWN STYLE OF JUMP BLUES THAT JUST SORT OF GETS YOU SHAKIN' YOUR BOOTY AND STOMPIN' YOUR FEET. SOME OF MY FAVORITE BLUES JOINTS ARE KINGSTON MINES, BUDDY GUY'S LEGENDS, BLUE CHICAGO, CHECKERBOARD LOUNGE, ROSA'S, AND B.L.U.E.S. IN MY BOOK, THERE AIN'T TOO MUCH BETTER THAN LISTENING TO SOME BUTT-ROCKIN' BLUES WHILE YOU'RE EATING SOME HEAVENLY SMOKEY BARBEQUE WITH THE SAUCE RUNNING DOWN TO YOUR ELBOWS. TODAY, SOME OF MY FAVORITE CHICAGO RIB JOINTS ARE LEM'S, HECKY'S, AND THE RIB PALACE—STOREFRONT BARBEQUES RUN BY ON-SITE OWNERS WHO PAY ATTENTION TO THE QUALITY OF THEIR FOOD.

I'VE SPENT 25 YEARS SCOURING URBAN NEIGHBORHOODS FOR LOCAL JOINTS THAT CLAIM LEGENDARY STATUS. I'VE FOUND SOME PLACES WHERE THE FOOD WAS SO GOOD THAT IT LEFT ME WITH CRAVINGS SO STRONG, I JUST HAD TO DUPLICATE THE RECIPES. THIS SECTION EXPLORES BLUES JOINTS AND STOREFRONT RESTAURANTS TUCKED AWAY ON SIDESTREETS— THE PLACES WHERE AMERICA REALLY EATS.

They say sharing your secret barbeque recipe with another person is like sharing your wife with another man —no good ever comes of it.

Famous Dave's
Legendary Pit Barbeque Ribs

"Best Ribs in America"—Great American Rib Cookoff, Cleveland, Ohio

Rib Rub (makes 6 cups)

- 2 cups packed light brown sugar
- 1 cup kosher salt
- 3/4 cup sugar
- 1/2 cup garlic seasoning
- 1/4 cup chili powder
- 1/4 cup lemon pepper
- 1/4 cup onion salt
- 1/4 cup celery salt
- 2 tablespoons coarse ground black pepper
- 2 tablespoons whole celery seeds
- 1 teaspoon crushed cloves
- 1 tablespoon cayenne
- 1/2 cup Mrs. Dash original blend
- 1/4 cup salt

Ribs

- 2 (4- to 5-pound) racks spareribs
- 1/2 cup Italian salad dressing
- 1/2 teaspoon coarse ground black pepper
- 1/2 cup packed brown sugar
- 1 cup minced dried onion
- 1 cup Rib Rub
- 1 (20-ounce) bottle Famous Dave's BBQ sauce

First prepare rib rub by thoroughly mixing all rub ingredients. Store in airtight container. The night before smoking, trim your ribs of all excess fat. Place them in a large plastic bag and pour in Italian dressing to coat. Seal bag well. Refrigerate for 4 hours, turning occasionally. Remove and wipe dressing off. Sprinkle each rib with pepper then 1/4 cup of the brown sugar and 1/2 cup of the onion flakes. Wrap each rib in plastic and refrigerate overnight. The next morning remove from wrap and wipe sludge off ribs. Generously coat front and back of ribs with Rib Rub and using your hands, rub seasoning into meat and set aside. The smoking process will take 6 hours. Using a chimney charcoal starter get 15 briquettes red hot. Place coals on one end of grill and place 1 pound of green hickory around coals. Use water-soaked hickory chunks if you can't get fresh-cut hickory.

Keep internal temperature of the grill at 200 to 225 degrees. Add more charcoal and hickory chunks every hour as needed. Place ribs bone side down but not directly over hot coals. After 3 hours, remove ribs from grill and wrap in aluminum foil. Hold in covered grill at 180 to 200 degrees for 1 1/2 to 2 hours or until fork tender. Next build a real hot bed of coals over the entire bottom of grill. Be careful because this next step goes quickly. Place ribs back on grill to add char flavor. When meat becomes bubbly it is done. Make sure to char off bone side membrane

until it becomes papery and disintegrates. Slather with BBQ sauce. Let heat caramelize sauce. This caramelizing along with the charring and slow smoking is the secret to tender smokey ribs just like the Championship pitmasters used to do down in the Deep South. There are no short-cuts to this time-honored way of barbequing. **Yield: 5 to 6 servings**

I THINK PEOPLE WILL ALWAYS FIGHT OVER WHO HAS THE BEST CHILI OR SPAGHETTI SAUCE, BUT THERE ISN'T ANYTHING MORE SECRET OR HOTLY CONTESTED THAN WHO HAS THE BEST BARBEQUE SAUCE. EVERY YEAR THERE ARE NATIONALLY SANCTIONED BARBEQUE CONTESTS WHERE BARBEQUERS LIKE MYSELF COMPETE FOR THOUSANDS OF DOLLARS IN PRIZE MONEY. THESE BIG EVENTS ARE ATTENDED BY HUNDREDS OF THOUSANDS OF PEOPLE ALL EAGER TO SEE WHO HAS THE BEST BARBEQUE IN THE COUNTRY. SOME OF THE BIGGER CONTESTS ARE MEMPHIS IN MAY, THE AMERICAN ROYAL IN KANSAS CITY, THE JACK DANIELS INVITATIONAL, AND THE GREAT AMERICAN RIB BURN-OFF IN CLEVELAND. AS YOU CAN SEE BY MY LIST OF AWARDS, I'VE WON MY FAIR SHARE.

BARBEQUE IS TRULY AN AMERICAN EATING EXPERIENCE. IN FACT, THE TRUTH IS THAT BARBEQUE GOES ALL THE WAY BACK TO THE AMERICAN INDIANS. AS LEGEND HAS IT, A GROUP OF INDIANS HAD ROUNDED UP A BUNCH OF WILD PIGS AND HAD THEM TIED TO A TREE. LATER THAT EVENING WHILE THEY WERE IN THEIR TEPEES EATING SUPPER, A PORRIDGE MADE UP OF CORN SWEETENED WITH NATIVE SUGAR CANE, A HUGE STORM BLEW UP. HEARING A LOUD CRACK OF LIGHTENING THEY RAN OUTSIDE TO SEE THAT THE LIGHTENING HAD STRUCK THE TREE WHERE THEY HAD TIED THEIR PIGS. THE LIGHTENING HAD SPLIT THE TREE IN TWO AND SET IT ON FIRE, FALLING ON THE PIGS. THE INDIANS QUICKLY THREW THEIR PORRIDGE ON THE BURNING PIGS TO PUT OUT THE FIRE. THIS IS THE TRUTH ON HOW BARBEQUE CAME TO BE. WITH BOTH MY PARENTS BEING AMERICAN INDIAN, IT'S NO WONDER THAT MAKING GOOD BARBEQUE COMES NATURALLY TO ME AND IS THE SOURCE OF MY PASSION.

A GOOD BARBEQUE SAUCE IS TOUGH TO MAKE BECAUSE IT HAS SO MANY COMPLEX FLAVORS. IT IS SWEET YET SOUR, MILD, SPICY OR SO HOT IT WILL RIP YOUR HEAD OFF. A GOOD BARBEQUER SPENDS MANY YEARS DEVELOPING HIS CRAFT. AS FOR MYSELF, I'VE SPENT 25 YEARS DEVELOPING MY SAUCES. IT'S REALLY A BLESSING FROM GOD TO HAVE A PALATE THAT CAN TASTE ALL THE FLAVORS NEEDED TO MAKE A GOOD BARBEQUE SAUCE. IF YOU'RE REALLY GOOD, PEOPLE WILL DRIVE FOR MILES JUST TO SATISFY THEIR CRAVINGS. IT'S NOT SOMETHING YOU GIVE AWAY TO JUST ANYBODY. MOST RECIPES ARE SECRET AND HANDED DOWN GENERATION TO GENERATION ONLY TO FAMILY MEMBERS.

IN FACT, IN MY HOUSE WHEN IT COMES TIME TO MAKE THE FAMILY RECIPE, EVERYONE WHO AIN'T FAMILY IS KICKED OUT OF THE HOUSE INCLUDING THE DOG! ALL SHADES ARE PULLED AND THE DOORS BOLTED BEFORE THE SECRET RECIPE IS PULLED FROM THE FAMILY STRONGBOX. WE EVEN SHOP DIFFERENT GROCERY STORES FOR THE DIFFERENT INGREDIENTS SO NO ONE KNOWS FOR SURE WHAT GOES INTO MY SAUCES! COMMERCIALLY WHEN WE MAKE SAUCES FOR MY RESTAURANTS, WE HAVE TWO DIFFERENT COMPANIES BLEND THE RECIPE. ONE COMPANY MAKES THE SPICE BLEND AND THE OTHER COMPANY BLENDS THE LIQUIDS—THAT'S HOW IMPORTANT IT IS TO PROTECT OUR SECRET SAUCES!

WHILE I HAVEN'T EXACTLY GIVEN YOU THE SECRET RECIPE FOR MY AWARD-WINNING SAUCES, I HAVE GIVEN YOU ONE THAT'S PRETTY GOOD. ONCE YOU MAKE IT YOU WILL APPRECIATE WHY MOST RECIPES ARE KEPT SECRET. BUT GOING THROUGH THE STEPS WILL, I HOPE, ENCOURAGE YOU TO TRY OUT DIFFERENT INGREDIENTS TO COME UP WITH YOUR OWN SECRET RECIPE.

Lip Smackin' Good
BBQ Sauce

2 thick strips hickory-smoked bacon
1/3 cup chopped sweet onion
1/4 cup water
3/4 cup peach schnapps
1/2 cup baking raisins
1 large jalapeño, finely diced
2 large cloves of garlic, minced
1/3 cup aged Alessi balsamic vinegar
1/4 cup chopped sweet apple
1/4 cup frozen tangerine juice
  concentrate
1/4 cup frozen pineapple juice
  concentrate
3 tablespoons molasses
2 tablespoons apple cider vinegar

2 tablespoons fresh lemon juice
2 tablespoons fresh lime juice
2 1/4 cups dark corn syrup
1 (12-ounce) can tomato paste
1/2 cup packed light brown sugar
1/2 cup Worcestershire sauce
2 tablespoons prepared mustard
2 teaspoons chili powder
1 teaspoon Maggi Seasoning
1 teaspoon salt
1/2 teaspoon crushed red pepper flakes
1/4 teaspoon coarse ground black pepper
1/4 teaspoon cayenne
1/4 cup Kahlúa
1 teaspoon liquid hickory smoke

Fry bacon in a large saucepan until crisp. Drain, reserving 1 tablespoon of the drippings. Eat the bacon. Fry onion in the reserved drippings over medium-high heat until caramelized or dark golden brown; do not burn. Reduce heat to medium-low. Deglaze saucepan with the water. Stir in peach schnapps, raisins, jalapeño and garlic. Simmer for 10 minutes or until the mixture is of a syrupy consistency, stirring occasionally. Remove from heat and place the mixture in a blender with the balsamic vinegar, apple, tangerine juice concentrate, pineapple juice concentrate, molasses, apple cider vinegar, lemon juice and lime juice. Process until puréed and return to saucepan. Add corn syrup, tomato paste, brown sugar, Worcestershire sauce, mustard, chili powder, Maggi Seasoning, salt, red pepper flakes, black pepper and cayenne and mix well. Bring to a low boil over medium heat, stirring frequently. Reduce heat to low. Simmer for 20 minutes, stirring occasionally. Remove from heat. Stir in Kahlúa and liquid smoke. Store, covered, in the refrigerator. **Yield: 4 cups**

CAUTION: THE SURGEON GENERAL HAS DETERMINED THAT SMOKING THIS SAUCE MAY HAVE APHRODISIAC SIDE EFFECTS. IT MAY CAUSE GIRLS TO BECOME SWEETER AND PRETTIER, BOYS TO BECOME TALLER AND HANDSOMER, OR VICE VERSA!

"I'VE GOT MY MOJO WORKING…"

Voodoo

VOODOO CHICKEN & MOJO SALSA

Mojo Salsa

¹/₃ cup each finely chopped green,
red and yellow bell peppers
¹/₃ cup chopped red onion
2 tablespoons butter
1 (8-ounce) can black beans, drained
8 ounces frozen corn kernels
¹/₄ cup frozen tangerine juice concentrate
1 large jalapeño, seeded, finely minced
2 tablespoons fresh lime juice
1 tablespoon chopped fresh cilantro
1 teaspoon red pepper flakes
¹/₄ teaspoon salt
¹/₄ teaspoon coarse ground black pepper

2 medium bananas, chopped
1 (8-ounce) can juice-pack pineapple chunks

Blackened Chicken

8 chicken breast halves
1 (16-ounce) bottle Italian salad dressing
Cajun Dynamite Dust (page 26)
2 tablespoons butter
"Whoop That Sweet Thang" Sweet & Sour
    Sauce (page 18)
8 cups cooked rice
Crossroads Delta Black Beans (page 19)

For the salsa, sauté bell peppers and onion in butter in a large saucepan just until onion is tender. Stir in black beans, corn, tangerine juice concentrate, jalapeño, lime juice, cilantro, red pepper flakes, salt and black pepper. Bring to a simmer. Stir in bananas and pineapple. Remove from heat. For the chicken, combine chicken and salad dressing in a shallow dish and mix well. Marinate, covered, in refrigerator for 2 hours or longer, turning occasionally; drain. Spoon about ¹/₃ cup of the Cajun seasoning on a large plate. Dust each chicken breast lightly with the seasoning on both sides. Heat a cast-iron skillet over high heat until hot. Add butter. Sauté chicken in butter until blackened and cooked through. Remove chicken to a platter. Brush with the Sweet & Sour Sauce. Spoon 1 cup of the rice on each of 8 plates. Layer each serving of rice with 1 cup of the black beans. Top with chicken. Serve with Mojo Salsa. Yield: 8 servings

Chicken

"Whoop That Sweet Thang" Sweet & Sour Sauce

1¹/₂ tablespoons cornstarch
1 cup pineapple juice
¹/₂ cup frozen tangerine juice concentrate
¹/₂ cup Polaner apricot preserves
¹/₄ cup sugar
2 tablespoons white vinegar
¹/₄ teaspoon salt
¹/₂ teaspoon crushed red pepper flakes
2 teaspoons Famous Dave's Chickn' Wing seasoning
2 tablespoons fresh lime juice

Mix cornstarch with pineapple juice until smooth. Mix in tangerine juice concentrate, apricot preserves, sugar, white vinegar, salt, pepper flakes and Chickn' Wing seasoning. Slowly bring to a low boil and simmer for 1 minute, stirring constantly. When sauce thickens remove from heat and add lime juice. Stir well and cool.
Yield: 2 cups

Crossroads Delta Black Beans

2 pounds dried black beans
3 quarts chicken stock
2 green bell peppers, cut into quarters
4 bay leaves
2 pounds smoked pork hocks
¹/₄ teaspoon cayenne
¹/₂ bunch cilantro, coarsely chopped
2 white onions, chopped
1 green bell pepper, chopped
1 red bell pepper, chopped
2 large jalapeños, finely minced

¹/₄ cup bacon drippings
2 tablespoons chopped fresh basil
1 tablespoon ground cumin
¹/₄ cup minced garlic
¹/₂ cup bacon drippings
2 tablespoons Famous Dave's
  BBQ sauce
2 tablespoons Kahlúa
2 teaspoons lime juice
1 teaspoon kosher salt
12 servings hot cooked rice

Sort and rinse the beans. Combine beans, stock, 2 quartered green peppers, bay leaves, pork hocks and cayenne in stockpot. Bring to a low simmer; skim foam. Stir in cilantro. Simmer, covered, for 1¹/₂ to 2 hours or until the beans are almost tender, stirring occasionally. Discard green peppers and bay leaves. Remove pork hocks and debone. Return meat to beans. Sauté onions, 1 green pepper, red pepper and jalapeños in ¹/₄ cup bacon drippings in a skillet just until the onions are tender. Stir in basil and cumin. Remove from heat. Sauté garlic in ¹/₂ cup bacon drippings in a saucepan until golden brown. Strain the beans, reserving the stock; set the beans aside. Stir the onion mixture and garlic into the stock. Add BBQ sauce, Kahlúa, lime juice and kosher salt. Process the stock mixture in a blender until puréed. Combine with the beans and meat in stockpot. Simmer for 5 minutes, stirring occasionally. Remove from heat. Chill, covered, for 8 to 10 hours to allow the flavors to fully blossom. Reheat over low heat, stirring frequently. Serve over hot cooked rice. **Yield: 12 servings**

New Orleans
Jazz Brunch

Seafood Newboogie

2 cups water
1 tablespoon seafood base
1/3 cup butter
2/3 cup flour
2 cups heavy whipping cream
4 egg yolks, beaten
1 1/2 teaspoons Old Bay seasoning
1 teaspoon dry mustard
1 teaspoon salt
1/2 teaspoon nutmeg
1/2 teaspoon Hungarian paprika

1/8 teaspoon cayenne
1 cup chopped cooked lobster
1 cup chopped cooked shrimp
1 cup chopped scallops,
   sautéed in butter
1 cup lump crab meat
1/3 cup cream sherry
6 cups cooked rice
3/4 cup shredded Monterey
   Jack cheese
Paprika to taste

Mix water and seafood base in a small bowl. Set aside. Heat butter in a saucepan until melted. Stir in flour. Cook over low heat for 2 to 3 minutes, stirring constantly; do not brown. Add seafood base mixture gradually, stirring constantly. Stir in whipping cream, egg yolks, Old Bay seasoning, dry mustard, salt, nutmeg, 1/2 teaspoon paprika and cayenne. Bring to a simmer over low heat, stirring constantly. Stir in lobster, shrimp, scallops and crab meat. Bring to a simmer, stirring frequently. Remove from heat. Stir in sherry. Preheat the broiler. Spread the rice over the bottoms of 6 individual au gratin dishes. Spoon the seafood mixture over the rice. Sprinkle with the cheese. Broil until light golden brown and bubbly. Sprinkle with paprika to taste. Serve immediately with garlic toast. May substitute a mixture of 1 cup seafood stock and 1 cup liebfraumilch for 2 cups seafood stock.
Yield: 6 servings

Sassy Mae's Chowder

½ cup plus 2 tablespoons butter
1 cup flour
1 gallon water
¾ cup lobster or seafood base
1 cup minced fresh clams
1 cup lump crab meat, shells removed
1½ cups chardonnay
1½ cups liebfraumilch
¼ cup lemon juice
2 cups frozen corn niblets
1½ cups finely chopped onions
1½ cups finely chopped celery
1½ cups finely chopped potatoes

1 green bell pepper, finely chopped
1 red bell pepper, finely chopped
1 jalapeño, finely chopped
2 tablespoons Worcestershire sauce
2 tablespoons Famous Dave's BBQ sauce
2 tablespoons tomato paste
1 tablespoon Famous Dave's Steak seasoning
1 tablespoon Old Bay seasoning
1 teaspoon chili powder
1 teaspoon cumin
1 teaspoon crushed red pepper flakes
2 cups heavy whipping cream
1 tablespoon finely chopped parsley

For the roux, heat butter in a heavy saucepan over medium heat until melted. Add flour, stirring until blended; reduce heat. Simmer for 2 minutes, stirring constantly; do not brown. Set aside. For the chowder, mix water and lobster base in a stockpot. Bring to a low rolling boil. Stir in clams and crab meat; reduce heat to simmer. Mix in wine and lemon juice. Add corn, onions, celery, potatoes, green pepper, red pepper and jalapeño. Cook for 8 minutes or until the vegetables are tender-crisp. Remove the clams, crab meat and vegetables to a food processor with a slotted spoon. Pulse several times to break up the mixture; do not purée. Set aside. Stir the roux into the stock. Add the Worcestershire sauce, BBQ sauce, tomato paste, steak seasoning, Old Bay seasoning, chili powder, cumin and red pepper flakes and mix well. Simmer for 20 minutes, stirring occasionally. Add the processed vegetable and seafood mixture and mix well. Bring to a low rolling boil, stirring occasionally. Remove from heat. Stir in whipping cream and parsley. Ladle into soup bowls. Yield: 6 quarts

Muddy Waters' Crab Cakes

These ain't just any ol' namby-pamby crab cakes. These are spicy, down home, real good crab cakes, Southern-style!

1/4 cup small white corn niblets
1 scallion, finely chopped
2 cloves of garlic, finely minced
2 tablespoons butter
1/3 cup butter cracker crumbs
1/3 cup plain bread crumbs
1/3 cup Panko bread crumbs
1/2 cup grated Parmesan cheese
1/3 cup mayonnaise
1/4 cup finely chopped pimento
2 eggs, beaten
2 tablespoons chopped parsley

2 tablespoons finely minced seeded
  jalapeño
1 tablespoon fresh lemon juice
1 tablespoon Worcestershire sauce
1 teaspoon dry mustard
1 teaspoon Old Bay seasoning
1/4 teaspoon cayenne
1 pound lump crab meat
2 tablespoons butter
2 tablespoons peanut oil
Creole Stomp Tartar Sauce (page 29)

Process the corn in food processor in short bursts just until the niblets burst; do not purée. Set aside. Sauté scallion and garlic in 2 tablespoons butter in a skillet until tender. Let stand until cool. Mix cracker crumbs, bread crumbs and cheese in a bowl; set aside. In another bowl, combine the scallion mixture, mayonnaise, pimento, eggs, parsley, jalapeño, lemon juice, Worcestershire sauce, dry mustard, Old Bay seasoning and cayenne in a bowl and mix well. Stir in 1/3 of the cracker crumb mixture and corn. Fold in the crab meat. Chill, covered, for 8 to 10 hours. Shape the crab meat mixture into 8 patties. Coat with the remaining cracker crumb mixture. Heat 2 tablespoons butter and peanut oil in a skillet until hot. Sauté the patties in the butter mixture until golden brown on both sides; drain. Serve with lemon wedges and Creole Stomp Tartar Sauce. Yield: 8 servings

Silky Smooth Hollandaise Sauce & Crab Cakes Benedict

1 tablespoon finely chopped red onion
2 teaspoons minced fresh jalapeño
2 tablespoons cider vinegar
1/4 teaspoon crushed red pepper flakes
1/2 teaspoon red pepper sauce
1/4 cup water
6 egg yolks, beaten

1 pound unsalted butter, melted
1 tablespoon lemon juice
1/2 teaspoon Old Bay seasoning
1/4 teaspoon salt
1/8 teaspoon cayenne
8 poached eggs
8 Muddy Waters' Crab Cakes

Combine red onion, jalapeño, vinegar, red pepper flakes, red pepper sauce and water in a saucepan. Bring just to the simmering point over low heat. Cook until reduced by half. Add gradually to beaten egg yolks, mixing constantly. Place in double boiler over hot water. Cook and whisk constantly until soft peaks form. Remove from heat. Slowly drizzle butter while whisking constantly. Add lemon juice, Old Bay seasoning, salt and cayenne. Mix well. Place a poached egg on each crab cake. Top with hollandaise sauce. Yield: 8 servings

Cajun Zydeco Cha-Cha Catfish Platter

Cajun Dynamite Dust

$^1/_2$ cup paprika
6 tablespoons kosher salt
$^1/_4$ cup coarse ground black pepper
3 tablespoons dried basil
3 tablespoons filé powder
2 tablespoons garlic powder
2 tablespoons dry mustard
2 tablespoons onion powder
2 tablespoons dried oregano

2 tablespoons cayenne
2 tablespoons ground white pepper
2 tablespoons dried thyme

Blackened Catfish and Shrimp

1 cup Cajun Dynamite Dust
4 catfish fillets
12 peeled shrimp (26 to 30 count)
2 tablespoons unsalted butter
4 servings red beans and rice

For the Cajun seasoning, mix all ingredients in a bowl. Store in an airtight container in a dark cool environment. Use as rub for blackened dishes. For the blackened catfish and shrimp, place 1 cup of seasoning on a flat plate. Coat each catfish fillet and shrimp with seasoning. Using your hands, rub seasoning into the fillets and shrimp. Heat cast-iron skillet over high heat until very hot; add butter. Heat until sizzling. Add catfish. Pan-fry until blackened on both sides, turning once. Unless you have a high-draft commercial-type exhaust hood, pan-fry the catfish as directed over hot coals on a grill outside. Serve on a bed of red beans and rice. If your taste buds are sensitive, reduce cayenne by half.
Yield: 4 main dish servings and 2$^1/_2$ cups seasoning

There are two secrets to great red beans. Soaking your beans overnight then rinsing them in fresh water the next morning (can you guess why?) and using smoked ham hocks.

"I've Got My Red Beans Cooking!"

2 large smoked ham hocks
1 cup finely chopped onion
2 cloves of garlic, minced
2 tablespoons bacon drippings
2 pounds small red beans
1 (49-ounce) can Swanson chicken broth
1 teaspoon Famous Dave's Steak seasoning

¼ teaspoon coarse ground black pepper
2 tablespoons Famous Dave's BBQ sauce
2 tablespoons Famous Dave's
  Georgia Mustard sauce
1 tablespoon red pepper sauce

Place ham hocks in a large pot with enough cold water to cover. Bring to a boil; reduce heat. Simmer for 45 minutes; skim fat. Sauté onion and garlic in bacon drippings in a large Dutch oven until translucent. Add ham hocks, ham broth and soaked beans. Add chicken broth. Stir in the remaining ingredients. Bring to a boil; reduce heat. Simmer slowly until the ham hocks are tender, adding water as necessary and stirring frequently. Serve over white rice. Yield: 16 servings

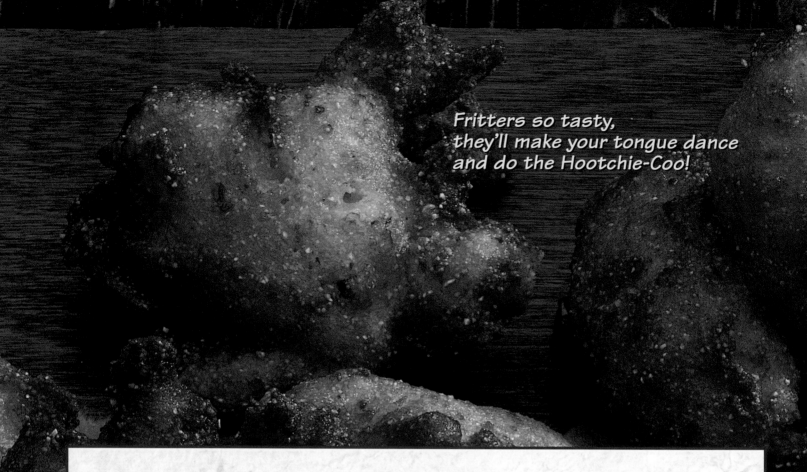

*Fritters so tasty,
they'll make your tongue dance
and do the Hootchie-Coo!*

Beale Street Shrimp and Corn Fritters

²/₃ cup yellow cornmeal
²/₃ cup stone-ground cornmeal
²/₃ cup flour
2 tablespoons sugar
2 teaspoons baking powder
1¹/₂ teaspoons salt
¹/₄ teaspoon cayenne
¹/₄ teaspoon black pepper

1 cup buttermilk
3 tablespoons peanut oil
1 egg, beaten
1 cup shrimp or crayfish pieces
1 cup sweet corn niblets
2 tablespoons chopped pimento
1 tablespoon finely diced jalapeño
Peanut oil for deep-frying

Combine cornmeals and flour together in a medium bowl and mix well. Add the remaining dry ingredients and mix well. Combine buttermilk, 3 tablespoons peanut oil and egg in a small bowl. Blend buttermilk mixture into cornmeal mixture; be careful not to over mix. Fold in shrimp, corn niblets, pimento and jalapeño. Pour peanut oil to ³/₄-inch depth in a heavy skillet. Heat over medium heat to 350 degrees. Don't get the oil too hot; it will brown your fritters too quickly. Drop fritters 1 full tablespoon at a time into the hot oil and deep-fry until the fritters are a deep golden brown. Drain on a wire rack positioned over a baking sheet and serve immediately with Creole Stomp Tartar Sauce. **Yield: 6 to 8 servings**

Creole Stomp Tartar Sauce

1¹/₂ cups mayonnaise
¹/₄ cup Famous Dave's BBQ sauce
1 tablespoon Old Bay seasoning
1 tablespoon lemon juice
2 teaspoons balsamic vinegar
2 teaspoons red pepper sauce
1 teaspoon cracked mixed peppercorns
¹/₂ teaspoon crushed red pepper flakes

1 cup finely chopped seeded tomato
1 cup finely chopped Granny Smith apple
¹/₂ cup finely chopped onion
¹/₄ cup finely chopped pimento
¹/₄ cup sweet pickle relish
1 jalapeño, seeded, finely minced
2 cloves of garlic, minced

Combine the mayonnaise, BBQ sauce, Old Bay seasoning, lemon juice, balsamic vinegar, red pepper sauce, peppercorns and red pepper flakes in a bowl and mix well. Stir in tomato, apple, onion, pimento, pickle relish, jalapeño and garlic. Store, covered, in refrigerator until serving time.

Yield: 5 cups

"Bangin' on the Keys" Lime Pie

Crust

1 cup graham cracker crumbs
$2/3$ cup gingersnap crumbs
6 tablespoons unsalted butter, softened
2 tablespoons light brown sugar
$3/4$ teaspoon grated Key lime or lime peel

Filling

6 egg yolks
$1^3/4$ cups sweetened condensed milk
$1/2$ cup Key lime juice
1 tablespoon lemon juice
2 teaspoons grated Key lime or lime peel
1 teaspoon grated lemon peel
$1/4$ teaspoon lemon oil
$1/8$ teaspoon salt

For the crust, combine graham cracker crumbs, gingersnap crumbs, butter, brown sugar and lime peel in a bowl. Mix until crumbs cling together to form a coarse mixture. Press crumb mixture over the bottom and up the side of a 9-inch pie plate. Chill in the refrigerator.

For the filling, preheat the oven to 325 degrees. Whisk egg yolks in a bowl until blended. Stir in condensed milk, lime juice, lemon juice, lime and lemon peel, lemon oil and salt. Pour into the prepared pie shell. Bake for 15 to 20 minutes or until set. Chill, covered, until serving time. Garnish with whipped cream and decorative lime slices just before serving. **Yield: 6 to 8 servings**

Finger Poppin' Honey Buffaloes

24 large chicken wings
3/4 cup hot sauce
1/4 cup French salad dressing
3 tablespoons honey
1 teaspoon crushed red pepper
1/2 teaspoon liquid smoke
3/4 teaspoon cayenne

1/4 teaspoon coarse ground black
  pepper
Peanut oil for frying
Dragon Wing Dust (page 62)
"Bluer Than Blooze" Cheese Dressing
Celery sticks

Smoke the chicken wings in a smoker at 225 degrees for 2 hours. Combine hot sauce, French salad dressing, honey, red pepper flakes, liquid smoke, cayenne and black pepper in a saucepan and mix well. Bring to a simmer, stirring occasionally. Remove from heat. Heat peanut oil in fryer to 375 degrees. Deep-fry smoked chicken wings in hot peanut oil for 5 to 6 minutes or until the wings rise to top. Fry for 1 minute longer; drain. Dust with wing dust. Toss with the hot sauce mixture in a bowl. Serve with blue cheese dressing and celery sticks. **Yield: 24 wings**

"Bluer Than Blooze" Cheese Dressing

2 cups mayonnaise
1 cup buttermilk
1 cup sour cream
4 ounces cream cheese, softened
1/2 cup finely chopped onion
2 tablespoons chopped fresh parsley
1 tablespoon lemon juice
2 teaspoons Worcestershire sauce

1 teaspoon red pepper sauce
1 teaspoon Famous Dave's Steak seasoning
1 teaspoon cracked pepper
1/2 teaspoon garlic powder
1 cup coarsely crumbled blue cheese
1/2 cup small curd cottage cheese
1/4 cup freshly grated Parmesan cheese

Combine mayonnaise, buttermilk, sour cream and cream cheese in a blender container. Process until smooth. Combine the mayonnaise mixture, onion, parsley, lemon juice, Worcestershire sauce, red pepper sauce, steak seasoning, pepper and garlic powder in a bowl and mix well. Fold in blue cheese, cottage cheese and Parmesan cheese. Chill, covered, until serving time or overnight to allow the flavors to marry. **Yield: 6 cups**

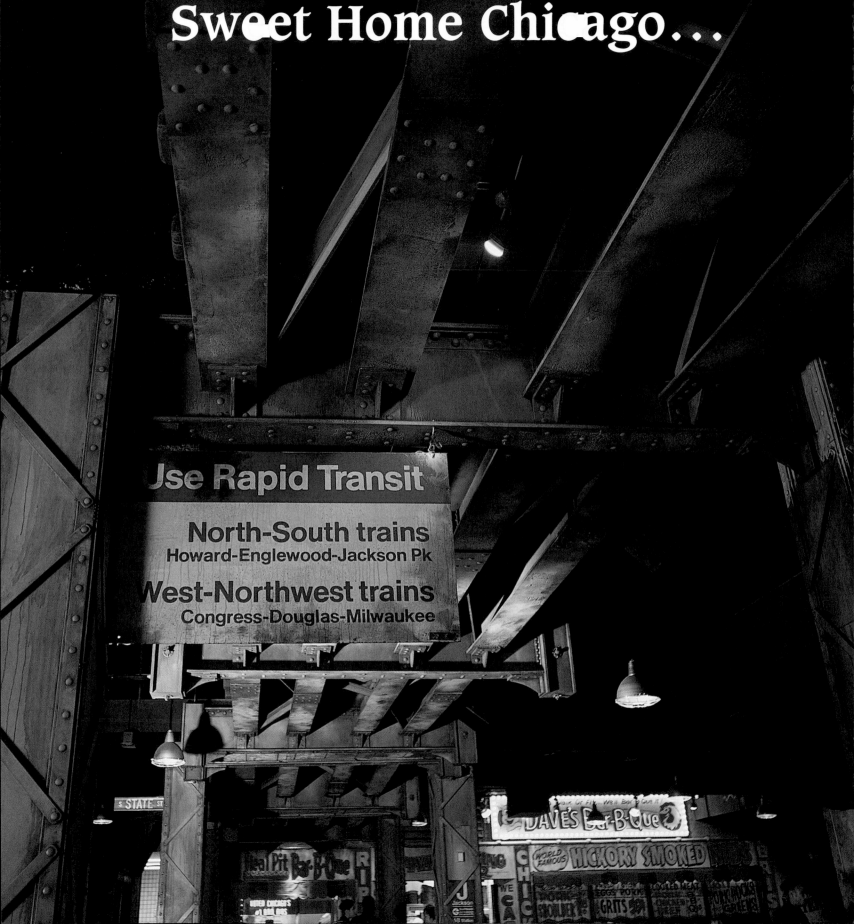

Sweet Home Chicago…

Blues Stew

1 pound hickory smoked bacon
1 pound hot Italian sausage
3/4 cup flour
2 (15-ounce) cans chicken broth
3½ quarts water
2 pounds beef, cubed
2 pounds pork, cubed
1 (4-pound) chicken fryer
2 (10-ounce) cans beef consommé
2 (15-ounce) cans diced tomatoes
2 finely minced jalapeños, seeded
2 cups sweet corn
2 cups chopped celery
2 cups chopped carrots
2 cups chopped onions
1 cup chopped green bell peppers
2 cups chopped potatoes
2 cups chopped green beans
2 teaspoons kosher salt
1/3 cup lemon juice
1/4 cup beef base
1 teaspoon chili powder
1 teaspoon Cajun seasoning
2 teaspoons horseradish
1 teaspoon crushed garlic
1/2 teaspoon coarse ground black pepper
1 cup Lea Perrins Worcestershire sauce
1/2 cup Famous Dave's BBQ sauce
1/2 cup Famous Dave's Texas Pit BBQ sauce

Cut bacon into 2-inch pieces. Place in large stockpot with sausage and fry until bacon is crisp. Remove bacon and sausage and set aside. To make roux, add flour to drippings and cook over high heat until flour browns. Remove from stockpot and set aside. To deglaze the pot, pour in 1 can chicken broth and stir over medium heat with whisk until glaze is removed from bottom of the pot. Add water, beef, pork and chicken and bring to a slow boil. Continue skimming off foam until stock turns clear. Cut up sausage into 1½-inch slices and add sausage and bacon to pot. Add chicken broth and beef consommé. Add remaining ingredients and cook for about 30 minutes or until vegetables are done. Bring to a boil and slowly stir in roux. Cook until stew thickens, stirring constantly. Yield: 20 servings

Kahlúa Fudge Brownies

1½ cups flour
½ cup baking cocoa
½ teaspoon baking powder
¼ teaspoon baking soda
½ teaspoon salt
1 cup semisweet chocolate chips
1 cup unsalted butter, softened

1 tablespoon vanilla extract
2 cups sugar
⅓ cup peanut oil
¼ cup espresso powder
4 eggs
1 cup chopped pecans
¼ cup Kahlúa

Mix flour, baking cocoa, baking powder, baking soda and salt in a bowl. Heat the chocolate chips and butter in a saucepan over low heat until blended, stirring frequently. Remove from heat. Stir in vanilla. Combine sugar, peanut oil, espresso and eggs in a mixer bowl. Beat for 5 minutes, scraping bowl occasionally. Add chocolate mixture. Beat just until blended. Add flour mixture, beating just until blended. Stir in pecans. Preheat the oven to 375 degrees. Spoon the batter into a buttered 9x13-inch baking pan. Bake for 25 to 30 minutes or until the edges pull from the sides of the pan; do not overbake. Cool to lukewarm on wire rack or just enough to handle pan. Pour Kahlúa into a clean spray bottle. Spray the warm brownies with the Kahlúa. Let stand until completely cool. To serve, cut into 3x4-inch brownies. Microwave just until warm. Split each bar into halves. Place the bottom half on a dessert plate and top with ice cream. Top with the remaining brownie half. Drizzle with warm fudge ice cream topping. Top with a dollop of whipped cream and fresh strawberries and/or raspberries. **Yield: 10 to 12 servings**

Snappy Green Beans

4 slices slab bacon
¹/₄ cup finely chopped onion
1 small jalapeño, seeded, finely minced
¹/₂ cup vinegar
3 tablespoons light brown sugar
2 tablespoons molasses
2 pounds fresh cut green beans, trimmed,
    diagonally sliced
2 teaspoons prepared horseradish
1 teaspoon salt
¹/₈ teaspoon coarse ground black pepper
¹/₈ teaspoon cayenne

Fry the bacon in a skillet until crisp. Drain, reserving 2 tablespoons of the drippings. Crumble the bacon, discarding the rind or save it to chew on. Sauté the onion and jalapeño in the reserved bacon drippings just until the onion is tender. Stir in the vinegar, brown sugar and molasses. Add the green beans, horseradish, salt, black pepper and cayenne. Bring to a simmer. Simmer, covered, for 15 minutes, stirring occasionally. Add the bacon. Cook, covered, for 5 minutes longer. Yield: 4 to 6 servings

Baked Apples and Cheese

1 cup packed light brown sugar
1 teaspoon cinnamon
2 tablespoons butter
4 cups sliced peeled
    Granny Smith apples
³/₄ cup flour
¹/₄ cup freshly grated
    Parmesan cheese
1¹/₂ cups sharp Cheddar cheese,
    cut into ¹/₂-inch cubes
2 cups Pecan Streusel
    Topping (page 87)

Mix brown sugar and cinnamon in a bowl. Cut in butter until crumbly. Stir in apples. Mix flour and Parmesan cheese in a bowl. Add sharp Cheddar cheese, tossing to coat. Add to apple mixture and mix well. Preheat the oven to 350 degrees. Spoon the apple mixture into a buttered 9x13-inch baking dish. Bake for 20 minutes. Lightly stir. Sprinkle with Pecan Streusel Topping. Bake for 10 minutes more. Yield: 5 to 6 servings

Grilled Blackened Pork Chops

4 (8-ounce) pork chops
1 quart Fried Chicken Marinade (page 108)
1/2 cup Cajun Dynamite Dust (page 26)

Pierce the pork chops with a fork. Place in a 2-gallon sealable plastic bag. Pour marinade over pork chops; seal tightly. Marinate in refrigerator for 8 hours, turning occasionally; drain. Return pork chops to refrigerator until ready to grill. Rub the Cajun Seasoning over both sides of pork chops. Grill over hot coals, turning several times; do not overcook. Yield: 4 servings.

Smokey Joe's Cafe BBQ Short Ribs

8 pounds beef short ribs
Famous Dave's Steak seasoning to taste
$\frac{1}{2}$ teaspoon coarse ground pepper
1 large onion, quartered, separated

1 (10-ounce) can beef consommé
2 cups Famous Dave's BBQ sauce
2 tablespoons sweet pickle relish

Preheat the oven to 300 degrees. Sprinkle the ribs generously on all sides with steak seasoning and the pepper. Place the ribs in a heavy roasting pan. Top with the onion. Pour the consommé around the ribs, being careful not to knock the seasonings off the ribs. Bake, covered, for 2$\frac{1}{2}$ hours. Remove the ribs to a platter; skim the fat from the juices. Remove the beef from the bones, discarding the bones. Return the beef to the pan. Pour a mixture of the BBQ sauce and pickle relish over the beef. Bake, covered, for 45 minutes; remove the cover. Bake for 15 minutes longer. Yield: 4 servings

Hot Jive Mashers

3 pounds unpeeled russet potatoes
2 quarts water
2 teaspoons kosher salt
$^{1}/_{2}$ cup heavy whipping cream
$^{1}/_{3}$ cup melted butter

$^{1}/_{3}$ cup Camembert cheese
1 teaspoon salt
$^{1}/_{4}$ teaspoon black pepper
$^{1}/_{4}$ teaspoon cayenne
$^{1}/_{8}$ teaspoon nutmeg

Slice the potatoes into halves; cut into quarters. Cut the quarters into halves. Bring water and kosher salt to a boil in a large saucepan. Add potatoes. Bring to a boil; reduce heat. Simmer for 15 minutes; drain. Mash the potatoes in a bowl. Heat whipping cream, butter and cheese in a saucepan until blended, stirring frequently; be careful not to boil. Remove from heat. Stir in 1 teaspoon salt, black pepper, cayenne and nutmeg. Add to the mashed potatoes and mix well. Yield: 6 servings

Secret Moppin' Sauce

3 (20-ounce) bottles Famous Dave's BBQ sauce
2 quarts water
1 cup beef stock base
1/4 cup Kahlúa
2 tablespoons yellow mustard
2 tablespoons blackstrap molasses
1 tablespoon liquid smoke
1 teaspoon toasted sesame seed oil
1 teaspoon coarse ground black pepper
1/2 teaspoon cayenne
1/2 teaspoon crushed red pepper flakes
2 sticks butter

Combine all ingredients in a stockpot and mix well. Simmer for 20 minutes, stirring occasionally.

Yield: 1 gallon

Jumpin', Juken' & Jiven All-Day Beef Brisket

Ask your butcher for a whole brisket and have him remove most of the fat, leaving only 1/4 inch to help preserve the juiciness during the cooking process. The brisket consists of two muscles: the flat and the point. The flat has less fat and will not be as flavorful, although it is very lean. Ask your butcher to separate the two muscles. Hand rub each brisket with 1 tablespoon fresh minced garlic and 1/2 cup of Rib Rub (page 13). Using the indirect smoking method as described in the rib recipe on page 13, start the smoking process. Smoke briskets for a minimum of 8 hours, keeping the temperature about 180 to 200 degrees. After 4 hours, to keep briskets from drying out, start mopping with Secret Moppin' Sauce every hour. At the end of 8 hours, briskets should be almost black. This wonderful blend of smoke, rib rub and Moppin' Sauce forms a crunchy exterior called "bark" on the briskets.

Most BBQ purists may disagree with this next step, but I have found most people who don't barbecue as often as I do will have a hard time controlling temperatures and almost always their brisket is tough. The following step will insure your brisket turns out very tasty, so tender grandpa can take out his teeth to eat! Wrap each brisket in a double layer of aluminum foil and pour 2 cups of Moppin' Sauce over brisket. Seal foil tightly and return to grill at 200 degrees for 3 hours. Remove briskets from aluminum foil and cool down. Once cool, wrap in plastic wrap and refrigerate overnight. Next day re-smoke over indirect heat at 225 to 235 degrees for 2 to 3 hours or until internal temperature reaches 160 degrees. Let stand for 15 minutes before slicing. Slice just before serving to preserve juiciness. Save the "burnt ends" for yourself, they're the best part! **Yield: 12 to 16 servings**

Garbage Can Salad

3 cups chopped iceberg lettuce
3 cups chopped romaine
2 cups chopped curly leaf lettuce
2 cups chopped curly endive
$1/2$ bunch parsley, tops only
2 cups charred chopped
   chicken breast
2 cups chopped tomatoes
1 cup crumbled bacon
1 cup shredded Monterey Jack cheese
$1/2$ cup crumbled blue cheese
$1/2$ cup sunflower seeds
$1/2$ cup chopped pecans
3 hard-boiled eggs, chopped
Blues Alley Buttermilk Dressing

Chop and toss the iceberg lettuce, romaine, curly leaf lettuce, endive and parsley in a large salad bowl. Add the chicken, tomatoes, bacon, Monterey Jack cheese, blue cheese, sunflower seeds, pecans and eggs and mix gently. Add the dressing and toss to coat. **Yield: 6 to 8 servings**

Blues Alley Buttermilk Dressing

3/4 cup French dressing
1/4 cup Famous Dave's BBQ sauce
1/3 cup finely crumbled blue cheese
1 tablespoon ranch salad dressing mix
1 teaspoon minced fresh jalapeño

1 teaspoon cracked mixed peppercorns
3/4 teaspoon Old Bay seasoning
1/4 teaspoon Famous Dave's Steak seasoning
1 1/4 cups buttermilk

Combine French dressing and BBQ sauce in a mixer bowl. Beat at low speed until blended. Add the blue cheese, salad dressing mix, jalapeño, peppercorns, Old Bay seasoning and steak seasoning and mix well. Add buttermilk gradually, beating constantly at low speed until mixed. Store, covered, in the refrigerator. **Yield: 2 1/2 cups**

ROADHOUSES & CAFÉS

One of the benefits of traveling a lot is stumbling upon great little roadside establishments, those community hangouts known only to truckers and road warriors like myself. After years of eating thousands of meals on the road (including a great many bad ones), I know exactly what to look for.

First, there are the billboard qualifiers: a hand-painted sign promising a family-owned restaurant that's been in business for generations, featuring home-cooked meals from scratch. I especially look for exaggerated boasts of "the best fried chicken in the world!" or "homemade pies better than grandma's." When I pull up, likely I'll see a conglomeration of buildings — tavern, gas station, and kitchen — looking like they were slapped together as the business expanded. And I know that I've really found a roadside treasure when I see a smokehouse out back with thick billowing smoke seeping through every crack.

I'm not impressed with new — old Formica tables, a mixture of vinyl and wood chairs, and mismatched silverware are just fine. It just means that they put more back into their cooking. In these little out-of-the-way places, waitresses, who have been there forever and know everyone by name, are capable of solving world problems and are just as quick to sass you back.

You can tell they're proud to serve up the best chicken and dumplings, hot barbeque sandwiches, lemon meringue pie, and coffee that always seems hotter and fresher. And if you came back tomorrow, everyone would still be sitting there in the same ol' seat, just like one big family — still gossiping about each other!

I can always tell how good a restaurant is — right from the get-go — just by the quality of their soup and bread. If a restaurant has a good hearty homemade soup and fresh bread served with cold butter, you can be sure a good tasty home-cooked meal is on the way. Today, when so many restaurants serve food that comes frozen in a plastic bag and warmed in a microwave, these roadside ma and pa's are the last bastions of real home cooking. This section is dedicated to these roadhouse kitchens.

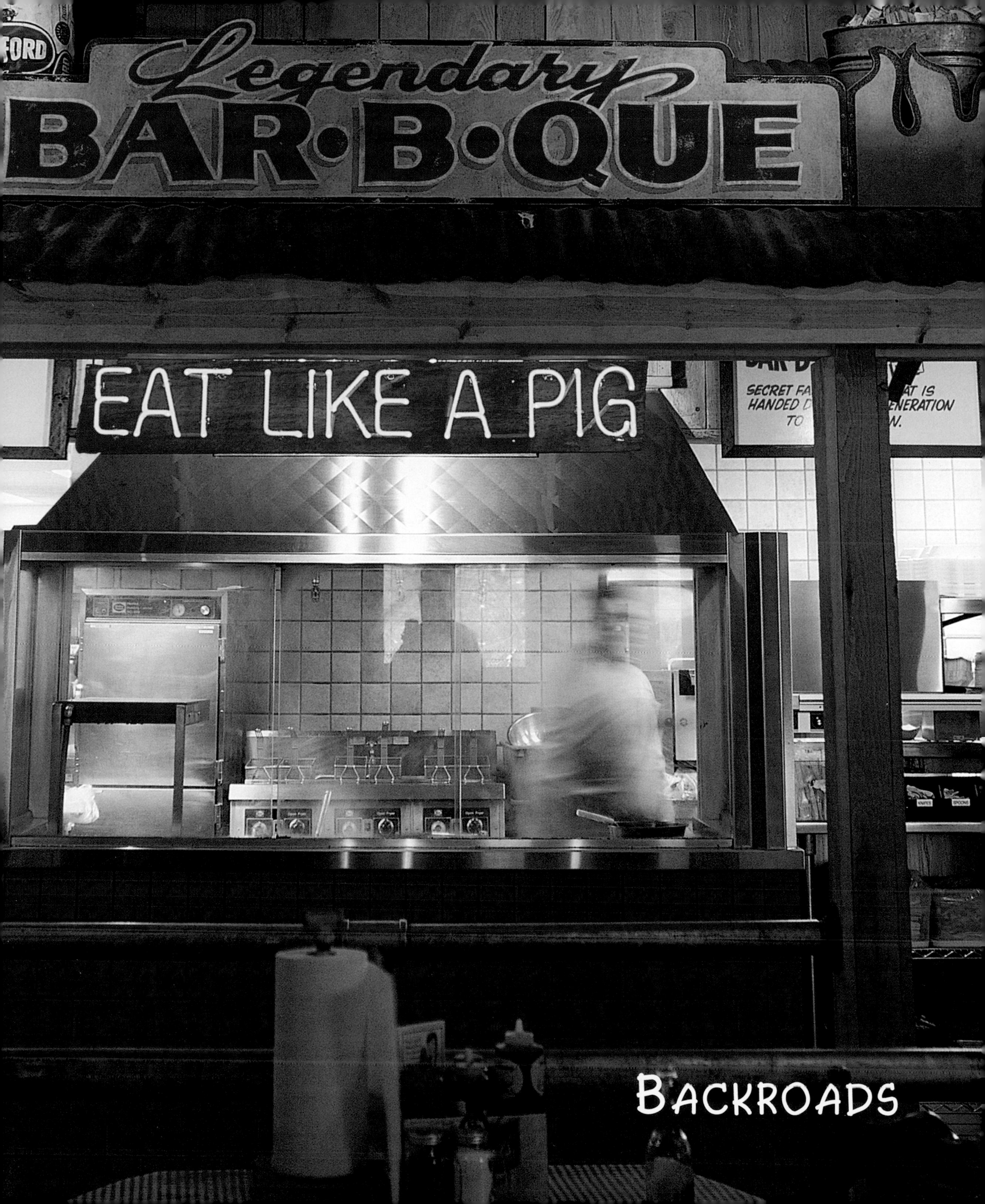

Backroads

Raisin Sauce for Country Ham

¹/₄ cup dark raisins

¹/₄ cup golden raisins

1 cup pineapple juice

¹/₄ cup frozen tangerine
   juice concentrate

1 tablespoon molasses

2 tablespoons Koops
   Dusseldorf Mustard

¹/₂ cup packed light brown sugar

¹/₂ teaspoon cinnamon

10 whole cloves

1 tablespoon fresh lemon juice

1 tablespoon cider vinegar

4 teaspoons cornstarch

¹/₄ cup water

Mix raisins, pineapple juice, tangerine juice concentrate, molasses, mustard, brown sugar, cinnamon, cloves, lemon juice and vinegar together in a saucepan. Cook over low heat until raisins plump. Mix cornstarch and water together and add to raisin mixture. Increase heat to medium to bring sauce to a boil. Cook until sauce thickens, stirring constantly. Remove from heat and remove cloves. Serve over fried country ham with cheesy grits and roadhouse fries. **Yield: 2 cups**

Front Porch Cheesy Grits

4 cups water
1 teaspoon salt
1 cup uncooked regular grits
1 cup shredded mild Cheddar
  cheese
6 ounces Velveeta cheese
1/2 cup butter
1/4 cup heavy whipping cream
3 eggs, beaten

Bring the water and salt to a boil in a saucepan over high heat. Add grits gradually, stirring constantly; reduce heat. Simmer, covered, over low heat for 15 minutes or until thickened, stirring occasionally. Add 1/2 cup Cheddar cheese, Velveeta cheese and butter and mix well. Remove from heat. Preheat the oven to 350 degrees. Whisk whipping cream and eggs in a bowl until blended. Stir into the grits. Spoon into a buttered 2-quart baking dish. Bake for 50 minutes. Sprinkle with 1/2 cup Cheddar cheese. Bake for 10 minutes longer. **Yield: 6 to 8 servings**

American Roadhouse Fries

3 pounds unpeeled russet potatoes
12 ounces smoked sausage
1/2 cup butter
1 small green bell pepper, coarsely chopped
1 small red bell pepper, coarsely chopped
1 small onion, coarsely chopped
2 teaspoons Mrs. Dash vegetable
  seasoning
1 teaspoon kosher salt
1/4 teaspoon coarse ground pepper
12 ounces smoked beef brisket, coarsely
  chopped

The night before, scrub potatoes and boil for 15 minutes. Refrigerate. The next day, smoke a smoked sausage for 2 hours at 175 degrees. A smoked sausage always tastes better if you smoke it again at home. Char-grill and rough chop the sausage. Remove potatoes from the refrigerator, quarter and slice. Sauté in 1/4 cup butter in a skillet. In another pan, sauté vegetables in the remaining 1/4 cup butter until just translucent. Add to potatoes and add seasonings. Add brisket and sausage. Serve in large casserole. **Yield: 6 to 8 servings**

Route 66 Truck Stop Chili

3 pounds (80/20) coarse ground beef
2 teaspoons Famous Dave's Steak seasoning
¼ cup plus 1 tablespoon chili powder
1 teaspoon coarse ground black pepper
4 teaspoons ground cumin
2 teaspoons Maggi Seasoning
1 tablespoon basil
1 teaspoon garlic powder
1 cup chopped celery
1 cup chopped onion
1 cup chopped green bell pepper
1 large jalapeño, finely chopped
2 (16-ounce) cans hot chili beans
1 (22-ounce) can tomato juice
1 (15-ounce) can diced tomatoes
1 (15-ounce) can tomato purée
1 (10-ounce) can beef broth
3 tablespoons Famous Dave's BBQ sauce
2 tablespoons Kahlúa
2 tablespoons Worcestershire sauce

Combine ground beef, steak seasoning, chili powder, black pepper, cumin, Maggi, basil and garlic powder in a stockpot and mix well. Cook until the ground beef begins to turn a crusty brown, stirring frequently. Add celery, onion, green pepper and jalapeño. Cook until the vegetables are tender, stirring frequently. Add undrained chili beans, tomato juice, undrained tomatoes, tomato purée, broth, BBQ sauce, Kahlúa and Worcestershire sauce and mix well. Simmer until the desired consistency, stirring occasionally. Ladle into chili bowls. Serve with shredded Cheddar cheese, minced onion, corn bread and/or crackers.

Yield: 6 to 8 servings

Smokin' Pork Shoulder Sandwiches

1 whole pork shoulder
Rib Rub (page 13)

The Colonel's Secret Mustard BBQ Sop
(page 57)

Order a whole pork shoulder from your butcher. There will be a thick skin on it which you'll have to cut off. Be careful to leave about 1/4 to 1/3 inch of fat on the shoulder. Rub a whole cup of Rib Rub into the shoulder using your hands. Slow smoke the shoulder for 6 to 8 hours depending on the size. Use the indirect heat method as described on page 13 for the spareribs. Internal temperature of your grill should be about 225 degrees. After smoking wrap the shoulder in aluminum foil and put back in your smoker over very low heat (180 to 200 degrees). Hold for 2 to 3 hours or until fork tender. The bone in the shoulder should fall right out. Pull meat apart with big grill forks. Leave as much of the smokey-black fat as possible (This is where all the flavor is!), only remove large white fat. Next chop up meat and sprinkle extra Rib Rub on meat to taste. Slather with mustard barbeque sop. Top with Creamy Sweet & Sour Coleslaw and serve on a toasted buttered bun with pickled peppers. **Yield: 10 to 12 sandwiches**

Creamy Sweet & Sour Coleslaw

10 cups chopped shredded red and green cabbage
¼ cup grated carrot
2 cups Miracle Whip
½ cup sugar
2 tablespoons prepared horseradish

1 tablespoon dry mustard
1 teaspoon white pepper
½ teaspoon salt
¼ teaspoon garlic powder
¼ teaspoon celery seeds

Toss the cabbage and carrot in a bowl. Mix salad dressing, sugar, horseradish, dry mustard, white pepper, salt, garlic powder and celery seeds in a bowl. Add to cabbage mixture and mix well. Chill, covered, until serving time. **Yield: 6 to 8 servings**

Sloppy Ques

1 pound ground beef
1/2 cup finely chopped sweet yellow onion
1/4 cup finely chopped green bell pepper
1 jalapeño, finely minced
1 teaspoon Famous Dave's
   Steak seasoning

1 tablespoon chili powder
1/4 teaspoon cayenne
1 1/2 cups Famous Dave's BBQ sauce
1 teaspoon prepared mustard
4 hamburger buns, split,
   buttered, toasted

Cook the ground beef in a skillet until the ground beef begins to brown; drain. Stir in onion, green pepper, jalapeño, steak seasoning and chili powder. Cook until the ground beef is cooked through and crumbly, stirring constantly. Add cayenne, sauce and mustard and mix well. Cook until heated through. Spoon onto the buns.

Yield: 4 servings

Hoe Cakes & Chopped Pork

2 cups white cornmeal
$^1/_3$ cup flour
1 teaspoon salt
2 cups boiling water
Shortening for frying

4 cups chopped smoked
 pork shoulder
The Colonel's Secret Mustard
 BBQ Sop
2 cups coleslaw

Combine the cornmeal, flour and salt in a bowl and mix well. Add the boiling water gradually, stirring constantly until mixed. Clean your hoe and get it good and hot over an open fire, or if that ain't yer cup of tea, a cast-iron skillet will do just fine. Heat the skillet until hot and add a small amount of shortening. Add enough of the hoe cake batter to make a 4-inch pancake. Cook until brown on both sides, turning once. Serve the hoe cakes with chopped smoked pork shoulder, mustard barbeque sop and coleslaw.
Yield: 8 to 10 servings

The Colonel's Secret Mustard BBQ Sop

1 cup apple cider vinegar
$^1/_4$ cup prepared yellow mustard
$^1/_4$ cup Worcestershire sauce
1 tablespoon sugar

$1^1/_2$ teaspoons salt
1 teaspoon chili powder
$^1/_2$ teaspoon black pepper
$^1/_4$ teaspoon cayenne

Combine the cider vinegar, prepared mustard, Worcestershire sauce, sugar, salt, chili powder, black pepper and cayenne in a saucepan and mix well. Simmer, covered, for 15 minutes, stirring occasionally. Store, covered, in the refrigerator. **Yield: 1 cup**

Dixie's Watermelon Punch

1 large watermelon
1/2 cup tangerine juice concentrate
1/2 cup cranberry juice concentrate
3 tablespoons lime juice

1/2 cup grenadine
1 quart lemon-lime soda
1 gallon rainbow sherbet

Slice a small piece off the bottom of the watermelon to level. Slice top from the watermelon and discard. Scoop out pulp, removing as many seeds as possible. Purée pulp in a blender and drain thoroughly in a colander, pressing purée to extract the juice. Measure 8 cups of the juice into a large pitcher. Add the tangerine and cranberry concentrates, lime juice and grenadine. Chill in the refrigerator. Cut the edge of the watermelon in a scallop pattern with a sharp knife to make a punch bowl. Wrap in plastic wrap. Chill until serving time. Add chilled lemon-lime soda to the watermelon juice and pour into the watermelon shell. Add scoops of sherbet just before serving. **Yield: 16 servings**

"Sweet Dreams" Chicken Fruit Salad

1 cup mayonnaise
1 cup sour cream
1 tablespoon French mustard
1 tablespoon balsamic vinegar
1 teaspoon salt
1/2 teaspoon white pepper
1/4 cup Claussen sweet pickle relish
1/2 cup slivered almonds
1/2 cup sunflower seeds
2 teaspoons butter
1 pound cooked chicken, chopped
1 cup chopped celery
3/4 cup chopped red onion
1 cup seedless green grape halves
1 cup drained pineapple pieces
1 cup drained Mandarin oranges
1 cup chopped Red Delicious apples

Make dressing by combining mayonnaise, sour cream, French mustard, vinegar, salt, pepper and pickle relish in a small bowl. Mix thoroughly. Toast almonds and sunflower seeds by placing in a shallow pan with 2 teaspoons butter in a 350-degree oven for 13 minutes. In a large bowl, combine chicken, celery, onion, grapes, pineapple, Mandarin oranges, chopped apples, almonds and sunflower seeds. Pour in dressing and toss. Serve on a bed of iceberg lettuce or in a watermelon shell. **Yield: 4 servings**

Fourth of July
Summertime Picnic

BACKROADS '61

Firecracker Wings

Dragon Wing Dust

2 tablespoons anise seeds
2 tablespoons salt
2 tablespoons Chinese 5 spice
2 tablespoons superfine sugar
1 tablespoon paprika
1 tablespoon garlic seasoning
2 teaspoons cayenne
2 teaspoons black pepper
1 teaspoon garlic powder

Wings

24 chicken wings
1 gallon Fried Chicken Marinade (page 108)
Peanut oil
4 cups flour
1 stick butter, melted
"Whoop That Sweet Thang" Sweet & Sour Sauce (page 16)

To make wing dust, grind anise seeds into powder in an electric coffee grinder. Mix next 8 ingredients together with anise powder. Grind this mixture again in coffee grinder and set aside. Wash wings. Place in marinade and refrigerate for 4 hours. Drain and discard marinade. Heat oil to 375 degrees in a heavy skillet. Oil should be about ³/₄ inch deep. Toss wings in flour until well coated. Turn heat to medium. Fry wings until golden brown. This takes about 12 to 15 minutes. Place wings on a sheet pan. Dip pastry brush into melted butter and dab on wings. Generously sprinkle with wing dust. Serve with Sweet & Sour Sauce. **Yield: 24 wings**

Rib-O'Licious Rib Tips

Rib tips are the cartilage and chine bone end of a full sparerib. It's a cheap piece of the rib that has been trimmed off. It is very meaty but also has a lot of fat running through it. However, rib tips can be very tasty and wonderful as a finger appetizer if they have been smoked long and slow. They are a true delicacy for all rib fanatics. Once the fat has been rendered out through the long smoking process, the remaining meat is succulent, very juicy, flavorful and tender. Actually I prefer rib tips over regular ribs.

Have your butcher reserve 10 pounds of rib tips. Rub them down with Rib Rub (page 13) and slow smoke according to the directions for smoking ribs (page 13). After they are smoked, char-grill them for additional flavoring and caramelize BBQ sauce on them. Using a cleaver and butcher block, chop them into bite-size pieces. Serve warm. **Yield: 6 to 8 servings**

Baby Back Sizzlers

8 pounds loin baby back ribs
32 ounces Robust Wishbone Italian Dressing
2 tablespoons hot pepper sauce
1 tablespoon crushed red pepper flakes
Chinese Dragon Sauce

Marinate ribs in mixture of Italian Dressing, hot pepper sauce and red pepper flakes in refrigerator for at least 8 hours. Smoke ribs at 225 degrees for 3 hours and cool. Cover with Dragon Sauce and refrigerate until ready to use. Char-grill and baste with Dragon Sauce. **Yield: 6 to 8 servings**

Chinese Dragon Sauce Combine in blender 2 cups frozen tangerine juice concentrate, 2 cups Kikkoman's teriyaki glaze, 1 cup light brown sugar, 1/4 cup spicy hot brown mustard, 1/4 cup sweet pickle relish, 1 teaspoon toasted sesame seed oil and 1 teaspoon liquid smoke. Lightly pulse to mix. Simmer in saucepan over low heat for 15 minutes before basting ribs.

Great Balls of Fire

Meatballs

3 pounds ground beef
3 eggs, beaten
1/2 cup heavy whipping cream
2 cups Ritz cracker crumbs
1/2 cup finely diced onion
1/3 cup finely diced green bell pepper
1/3 cup finely grated carrot

1 teaspoon salt
4 teaspoons Famous Dave's Steak seasoning
1 teaspoon Maggi Seasoning
1 teaspoon black pepper
2 teaspoons chili powder
2 teaspoons Dijon mustard
2 tablespoons Famous Dave's BBQ sauce

Sauce

1 (20-ounce) bottle Famous Dave's BBQ sauce
2 (10-ounce) bottles Polaner apricot preserves
1/3 cup finely diced onion
1/4 cup finely diced jalapeño
1/2 teaspoon cayenne

Combine all ingredients for meatballs in a bowl. Mix thoroughly. Use a small ice cream scoop to form balls, dipping in cold water as needed so meatball mixture won't stick. Place meatballs on a sheet pan lined with baking parchment paper. Bake at 350 degrees for 1 hour. Combine sauce ingredients in a saucepan and heat over medium heat until vegetables are tender. Pour over meatballs. **Yield: 3 dozen**

Shakin' The Shack Potato Salad

3 pounds medium russet potatoes
1¼ cups mayonnaise
½ cup sour cream
1 tablespoon prepared mustard
1 tablespoon white vinegar
1 teaspoon salt
1 teaspoon sugar
½ teaspoon pepper

½ cup finely chopped celery
½ cup finely chopped red onion
½ cup finely chopped green bell pepper
2 tablespoons finely chopped pimento
1 tablespoon finely minced
    seeded jalapeño
5 hard-boiled eggs, finely chopped
¼ cup pickle relish

Combine the potatoes with enough water to cover in large saucepan. Bring to a boil. Boil until tender but not mushy; drain. Chill in refrigerator. Peel potatoes and coarsely chop. Combine mayonnaise, sour cream, mustard, vinegar, salt, sugar and pepper in a bowl and mix well. Stir in celery, red onion, green pepper, pimento and jalapeño. Fold in potatoes, eggs and pickle relish. Chill, covered, until serving time. The flavor is enhanced if chilled overnight. Garnish with paprika. **Yield: 10 to 12 servings**

Annie Girl's Picnic Corn Relish

²/₃ cup cider vinegar
¹/₃ cup packed brown sugar
1 teaspoon cornstarch
1 teaspoon salt
¹/₄ teaspoon coarse ground pepper
¹/₂ teaspoon mustard seeds

¹/₂ teaspoon celery seeds
3 cups sweet corn niblets
¹/₄ cup finely chopped green bell pepper
¹/₄ cup finely chopped sweet onion
¹/₄ cup chopped drained pimento
1 small jalapeño, seeded, finely minced

Combine vinegar, brown sugar, cornstarch, salt, pepper, mustard seeds and celery seeds in a saucepan and mix well. Bring to a boil; reduce heat. Simmer for 2 minutes, stirring occasionally. Remove from heat. Stir in corn, green pepper, onion, pimento and jalapeño. Let stand until cool. Chill, covered, until serving time. **Yield: 4 cups**

Lemon Apricot Bars

Crust

1^1/$_2$ cups flour
^{1}/$_2$ cup confectioners' sugar
^{3}/$_4$ cup unsalted butter, softened

Filling

^{1}/$_2$ cup apricot preserves
4 eggs
2 cups sugar
6 tablespoons lemon juice
1 tablespoon grated lemon peel
^{1}/$_4$ cup flour
1 teaspoon baking powder
^{1}/$_2$ teaspoon lemon oil
^{1}/$_2$ teaspoon salt
Confectioners' sugar to taste

For the crust, mix flour and confectioners' sugar in a bowl. Cut in butter until crumbly. Preheat the oven to 350 degrees. Press the crumb mixture over the bottom of 9x13-inch baking pan. Bake for 30 minutes. Let stand until cool. Reduce the oven temperature to 325 degrees.

For the filling, spread the apricot preserves over the bottom of the crust. Beat the eggs in a mixer bowl until blended. Add sugar, lemon juice, lemon peel, flour, baking powder, lemon oil and salt. Beat until blended. Pour over the prepared layers. Bake for 35 minutes. Let stand until cool. Sprinkle with confectioners' sugar. Cut into bars.

Yield: 36 bars

Smoky Mountain Ham Sandwich

4 ounces pit-smoked ham, sliced
2 slices raisin cinnamon bread
Spankin' Jalapeño Honey Mustard
2 slices smokey Cheddar cheese
2 tablespoons butter
Thinly sliced fresh apple

Grill the ham slices over hot coals. Spread one side of each of the bread slices with a thin layer of honey mustard and top with 1 slice of cheese. Heat butter in a skillet until melted. Arrange the bread slices cheese side up in the skillet. Cook until the bread begins to brown. Layer the ham and apple slices over the cheese on 1 slice. Top with the remaining bread slice. Cut into halves. **Yield: 1 serving**

Spankin' Jalapeño Honey Mustard

^{1}/2 cup Polish mustard or Dijon mustard
^{1}/2 cup French mustard (full seed)
^{1}/2 cup mayonnaise
^{1}/2 cup honey
1 small jalapeño, seeded, minced
1 teaspoon balsamic vinegar
^{1}/2 teaspoon cayenne

Combine Polish mustard, French mustard, mayonnaise, honey, jalapeño, balsamic vinegar and cayenne in a bowl and mix well. Store, covered, in the refrigerator. **Yield: 2 cups**

Sweet Potato Chips

3 large sweet potatoes and peanut oil

Scrub the sweet potatoes and pat dry. Cut into thin slices, about the thickness of a thick potato chip. Add enough peanut oil to a heavy skillet or Dutch oven to measure 1 inch. Heat to 375 degrees. Fry the sweet potatoes in the hot peanut oil until crisp; drain.
Yield: 4 servings

Pumpkin Wild Rice Soup

1 cup chopped celery
1 cup chopped onion
3 tablespoons butter
1 cup chicken stock
$\frac{1}{2}$ teaspoon salt
$\frac{1}{4}$ teaspoon ground nutmeg
$\frac{1}{4}$ teaspoon cinnamon
$\frac{1}{4}$ teaspoon black pepper
$\frac{1}{4}$ teaspoon cayenne
$\frac{1}{8}$ teaspoon white pepper
$\frac{1}{8}$ teaspoon ground cloves
$\frac{1}{8}$ teaspoon ginger
1 (29-ounce) can solid-pack pumpkin
4 cups chicken stock
2 cups cooked wild rice
$\frac{1}{4}$ cup grated carrot
1 cup heavy whipping cream
8 ounces Camembert cheese,
   rind removed and chopped
$\frac{1}{2}$ cup sunflower seeds,
   toasted in butter

Sauté celery and onion in butter in a large stockpot until tender. Add 1 cup stock. Bring to a boil. Process the stock mixture, salt, nutmeg, cinnamon, black pepper, cayenne, white pepper, cloves and ginger in a blender until puréed. Add pumpkin. Process until blended. Return the pumpkin mixture to stockpot. Add 4 cups stock, wild rice and carrot. Bring to a simmer, stirring occasionally. Simmer for 10 minutes, stirring occasionally. Stir in whipping cream and cheese. Cook until the cheese melts and the soup is heated through, stirring frequently. Add sunflower seeds and mix well. Ladle into soup bowls. **Yield: 10 servings**

The tastiest baked-bean recipe you'll ever try...no leftovers! Guaranteed!

Baked "Wilbur" Beans

8 ounces thick-slice hickory-smoked bacon
1 (8-ounce) strip steak
Famous Dave's Steak seasoning to taste
1 (8-ounce) twice-smoked sausage link
2 tablespoons bacon drippings
1 cup chopped onion

⅓ cup chopped green bell pepper
1 tablespoon diced jalapeño
2 (28-ounce) cans Bush's Baked Beans
1 (20-ounce) bottle Famous Dave's
   BBQ sauce

Fry bacon in a skillet until crisp. Drain, reserving 2 tablespoons of the drippings. Crumble the bacon. Sprinkle steak with steak seasoning. Grill over hot coals until medium. Cut into ½-inch cubes. Grill sausage until nice and charred. Slice the sausage lengthwise into halves; slice into quarters. Cut the quarters into ½-inch cubes. Sauté onion, green pepper and jalapeño in reserved bacon drippings in a skillet just until onion is tender-crisp. Stir in bacon, steak, sausage, beans and sauce. Simmer over low heat for 30 minutes, stirring occasionally. The flavor is enhanced if stored, covered, in the refrigerator for 8 to 10 hours and reheated just before serving. To resmoke sausage, smoke over hickory chips at 175 degrees for 2 hours. Grill over hot coals for additional flavor. **Yield: 12 to 15 servings**

Caraway Cheddar Cheese Soup

½ cup finely chopped onion
½ cup finely chopped celery
½ cup finely chopped carrot
1 fresh jalapeño, seeded, finely minced
¼ cup butter
2 teaspoons caraway seeds
3 tablespoons flour
4 cups chicken broth, heated
1 cup shredded sharp Cheddar cheese
1 cup Camembert cheese or domestic
   Brie cheese
1 tablespoon Worcestershire sauce
1 teaspoon dry mustard
½ teaspoon pepper
Sunflower seeds, toasted

Sauté onion, celery, carrot and jalapeño in butter in a stockpot until the onion is tender; do not brown. Stir in caraway seeds. Sprinkle with the flour and mix well. Cook for 2 minutes or or until of a roux consistency, stirring constantly. Add the heated broth gradually, stirring constantly. Simmer for 30 minutes, stirring occasionally. Process the vegetable mixture in a food processor until smooth. Return the vegetable mixture to stockpot. Add Cheddar cheese, Camembert cheese, Worcestershire sauce, dry mustard and pepper and mix well. Cook until the cheese melts, stirring constantly. Strain through cheesecloth into a bowl and discard vegetables. Return soup to stockpot. Simmer until heated through, stirring frequently. Ladle into soup bowls. Garnish with toasted sunflower seeds.
Yield: 6 to 8 servings

This delightful soup will warm any tummy on a chilly day. Camembert cheese adds wonderful, velvety texture to your palate.

Dairyland Mac and Cheese

Pasta

- 3 tablespoons flour
- 2 tablespoons butter, melted
- 2 cups milk
- 3/4 cup half-and-half
- 1 tablespoon Dijon mustard
- 2 teaspoons Famous Dave's BBQ sauce
- 1 teaspoon salt
- 1/4 teaspoon coarse ground pepper
- 4 ounces aged white Cheddar cheese, shredded
- 1/4 cup freshly grated Belgioioso Parmesan cheese
- 1 1/2 cups sweet corn niblets
- 2 jalapeños, finely chopped
- 1 tablespoon chopped fresh parsley
- 4 cups jumbo elbow macaroni, cooked
- 8 ounces sharp Cheddar cheese, cubed
- 8 ounces Colby cheese, cubed
- 1 1/2 cups small curd cottage cheese

Topping

- 1 cup butter cracker crumbs
- 1 cup Panko unseasoned bread crumbs
- 1/2 cup unseasoned bread crumbs
- 1/4 cup melted butter

Stir flour into butter in a saucepan until blended. Add mixture of milk and half-and-half gradually, stirring constantly. Stir in Dijon mustard, BBQ sauce, salt and pepper. Cook until thickened, stirring constantly. Add 4 ounces shredded white Cheddar cheese and grated Parmesan cheese and mix well. Cook until the cheese melts, stirring constantly. Stir in corn, jalapeños and parsley. Remove from heat. Combine sauce with macaroni, 8 ounces cubed Cheddar cheese, Colby cheese and cottage cheese in a bowl and mix gently. Spoon into a buttered 9x13-inch baking dish. Preheat the oven to 350 degrees. For the topping, mix cracker crumbs and bread crumbs in a bowl. Add butter gradually and toss to coat. Sprinkle the crumb mixture over the pasta mixture. Bake for 40 minutes or until brown and bubbly.

Yield: 8 to 10 servings

Famous Dave's Burgers

2 pounds (80/20) fresh ground beef
¼ cup chopped white onion
1 jalapeño, chopped
Famous Dave's BBQ sauce
2 teaspoons Famous Dave's Steak seasoning

¼ teaspoon coarse ground pepper
12 slices crisp-fried hickory-smoked bacon
4 slices smokey Cheddar cheese
4 hamburger buns, toasted, buttered
Tongue Slappin' Good Mustard Relish

Mix the ground beef, onion, jalapeño, 2 tablespoons BBQ sauce, steak seasoning and pepper in a bowl. Shape into 4 patties. Grill the patties over hot coals until medium-rare. Slather both sides of the patties with the BBQ sauce. Grill until desired degree of doneness, turning occasionally. The caramelizing of the sauce with the charring of the burgers creates a mouthwatering, addictive taste. Remove the patties from the grill. Preheat the broiler. Arrange the patties on a baking sheet. Top each with 3 slices of bacon and 1 slice of the cheese. Broil until the cheese melts. Serve on the buns with mustard relish. **Yield: 4 servings**

Famous French Fries

Russet potatoes   Rendered beef fat or peanut oil

Peel the potatoes and cut into fries. Combine the potatoes with enough cold water to cover in a bowl. Chill for 3 hours or longer; drain. For the best fries possible, use rendered beef fat, or use peanut oil if rendered beef fat is not an option. The secret to making really great fries is to fry them twice. The first deep-fry is the longest, about 8 minutes or until the fries are just turning a golden brown. The temperature of the oil must be 325 degrees exactly. Remove and drain. Fries may be kept for several hours before the final frying. It is important that they cool down first. Increase the temperature of the oil to 375 degrees for the second fry. Deep-fry for 2 minutes or until golden brown. This second fry is what makes them crunchy. Do not drain on paper towels. This is what causes the fries to become soggy. Drain on a wire rack positioned over a baking sheet. Sprinkle with salt and serve immediately.

Best Dang Buttermilk and Beer-Battered Onion Rings

1 cup sugar
2 quarts cold water
2 large sweet onions
1 cup cornmeal
3/4 cup flour
1/4 cup cornstarch
1 tablespoon onion powder

1/4 teaspoon salt
1/4 teaspoon cayenne
1 cup buttermilk
2 eggs, beaten
2 tablespoons peanut oil
1/3 cup good strong beer
Peanut oil for frying

Make sure to remove the membranes from between the onion rings; otherwise the batter won't stick!

Stir sugar into 2 quarts cold water. Slice onions 3/4 inch thick, place in sugar water and refrigerate. For the batter, mix all dry ingredients until well blended. Mix buttermilk, eggs and 2 tablespoons oil together and mix into cornmeal mixture. Lightly stir but do not over mix. Gently fold in the beer until well mixed. You can drink what's left of the beer. Refrigerate for 2 hours. Both rings and batter are best if chilled overnight. Drain onion rings. Make sure to discard thin membrane that separates from the rings. Place oil in a heavy skillet about 3/4 inch deep; heat to 350 degrees. Dip rings into batter and fry until a deep, dark golden brown. Drain on a wire rack.
Yield: 4 to 6 servings

Tongue Slappin' Good Mustard Relish

1 (10-ounce) jar Claussen Sweet Pickle Relish
1 cup chopped white onion
1 cup prepared yellow mustard

2 tablespoons chopped pimento
1/2 teaspoon coarse ground black pepper
1/8 teaspoon cayenne

Combine all ingredients in a bowl and mix well. Refrigerate until ready to use. **Yield: 3 1/2 cups**

Pineapple Upside-Down Cake

2/3 cup packed light brown sugar
1/3 cup unsalted butter, softened
1 teaspoon vanilla extract
1/2 teaspoon cinnamon
9 canned pineapple slices
9 maraschino cherry halves
2 egg yolks
1/2 cup sugar
1 1/2 cups flour

2 teaspoons baking powder
3/4 teaspoon salt
1/4 cup shortening
1/4 cup unsalted butter, softened
1/4 cup pineapple juice
1/4 cup half-and-half
1/4 cup buttermilk
1 teaspoon vanilla extract
2 egg whites, stiffly beaten

Preheat the oven to 350 degrees. Mix brown sugar and 1/3 cup butter in a bowl. Stir in 1 teaspoon vanilla and cinnamon. Spread evenly over the bottom of an ungreased 9-inch cast-iron skillet or 9x9-inch baking pan. Heat until the brown sugar melts. Arrange the pineapple slices over the brown sugar mixture. Place a cherry half in the middle of each slice. Beat egg yolks in a mixer bowl until thickened. Add 1/2 cup sugar gradually, beating constantly until blended. Mix flour, baking powder and salt in a mixer bowl. Add shortening, 1/4 cup butter, pineapple juice, half-and-half, buttermilk and 1 teaspoon vanilla. Beat until blended, scraping the bowl occasionally. Mix in egg yolk mixture. Fold in whipped egg whites. Spoon the batter into the prepared skillet. Bake for 35 to 40 minutes or until a wooden pick inserted in the center comes out clean. Invert the skillet onto a serving platter, allowing the skillet to rest on the cake for several minutes before removing.

Yield: 6 to 9 servings

If the fruit should stick to the skillet, just remove and rearrange back on top of the cake.

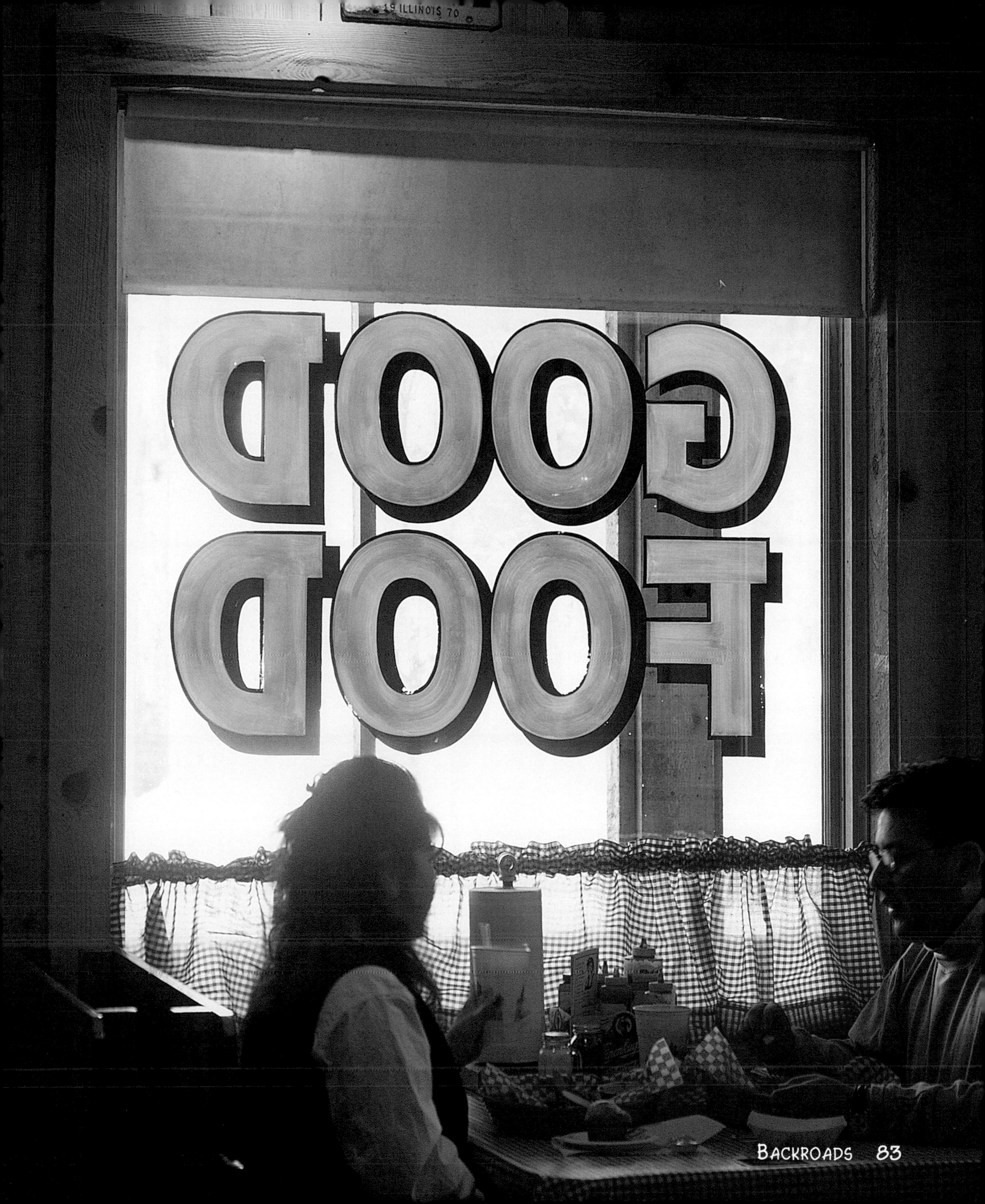
ILLINOIS 70
GOOD
FOOD

Country Kitchens

My dad, a Choctaw Indian, grew up in a small town, Idabel, located in the southeastern part of Oklahoma, right smack in the middle of the "Bible Belt." Although he and my mother lived in Chicago, he used to drive her down south every weekend until she learned how to cook southern! I learned something about how important the right ingredients are in making food taste good, because every so often he would have to travel down south for the red pepper sauce and homemade corn syrup he couldn't find in the stores up north.

Although we weren't exactly poor, my parents watched every dime and penny. But we always had good home-cooked meals on the table, especially because my parents were always inviting visiting missionaries over for Sunday dinner. I think that this was their way of saying thank you to God. Sunday afternoons after church were reserved for fried chicken, corn-on-the-cob, mashed potatoes and pan gravy, and corn bread served with plenty of honey. Most folks today don't know how tasty a tall, cold glass of fresh buttermilk mixed with crumbled corn bread can be.

My dad was very fond of old-fashioned gospel singing, southern style. We grew up listening to J.D. Sumner and the Stamps Quartet, The Blackwoods, The Singing Speer Family, and the Oak Ridge Boys before they went country. Other times, families would get together in the evening around an old upright and sing all their favorites: "I'll Fly Away," "Swing Low Sweet Chariot," "Will the Circle Be Unbroken," and "Amazing Grace," to name a few. Many times they would sing way into the night and it was almost morning before we'd go home.

The women would prepare casseroles of pork chops smothered in gravy, mashed sweet potatoes covered with melted marshmallows, sweet & sour cukes and onions, buttermilk yeast rolls, apricot fried pies, and sheet cakes. I grew up believing that Jesus was a Southerner and when he fed the multitudes, it was catfish and biscuits. As I grow older, I am grateful to have grown up where grace and abundance are so closely related. This section honors country kitchens and southern hospitality — no matter where.

Dusty Lanes

Country Mornings Raspberry Coffee Cake

½ cup sliced almonds
1 teaspoon butter
6 ounces cream cheese, softened
¼ cup unsalted butter
¼ cup buttermilk
1¼ cups sugar
2 eggs
1 teaspoon vanilla extract

2 cups flour
2 teaspoons baking powder
¾ teaspoon salt
3 cups chopped peeled apples (chop the size of nickels and pennies)
½ cup sugar
1 tablespoon cinnamon
1⅓ cups fresh raspberries

Preheat the oven to 350 degrees. Mix the almonds and 1 teaspoon butter in a bowl. Spread in a round baking dish. Toast for 13 minutes, stirring 1 or 2 times. Let stand until cool. Combine cream cheese, ¼ cup butter and buttermilk in a mixer bowl. Beat at low speed until creamy, scraping bowl occasionally. Whisk 1¼ cups sugar, eggs and vanilla in a bowl. Add to cream cheese mixture, beating until blended. Mix flour, baking powder and salt in a bowl. Add to cream cheese mixture. Beat at low speed until blended, scraping bowl occasionally. Toss apples with ½ cup sugar and cinnamon in a bowl. Fold into the batter. Spoon half the batter into a greased and floured bundt pan. Make a groove in the middle of the batter. Spoon half the Pecan Streusel topping in the groove. Top with the raspberries and remaining streusel topping. Spread with the remaining batter. Bake at 350 degrees for 1 hour or until the edge pulls from the side of the pan and a knife inserted in the middle comes out clean. Cool in pan on a wire rack for 25 minutes. Invert onto a serving platter. Spread with Cream Cheese Frosting and drizzle with Raspberry Glaze. Sprinkle with the almonds. **Yield: 16 servings**

Raspberry Glaze

1½ cups lightly packed fresh raspberries
½ cup sugar

½ cup water
1 tablespoon cornstarch
2 tablespoons water

Mix raspberries, sugar and ½ cup water in a saucepan. Bring to a boil and reduce by half, stirring occasionally. Strain, discarding seeds, and return to saucepan. Bring to a boil. Stir in a mixture of cornstarch and 2 tablespoons water. Boil until slightly thickened, stirring frequently. Cool to room temperature. **Yield: 2 cups**

Pecan Streusel

1/2 cup chopped pecans
1 teaspoon melted unsalted
    butter
2/3 cup flour
1/2 cup packed light brown sugar
1 teaspoon cinnamon
1/8 teaspoon ground nutmeg
1/2 cup unsalted butter

Toss the pecans with 1 teaspoon butter in a bowl. Spread in a round baking dish. Preheat the oven to 350 degrees. Bake for 13 minutes or until lightly toasted, then cool. Combine flour, brown sugar, cinnamon and nutmeg in a food processor container. Pulse in short bursts to mix. Add 1/2 cup butter. Pulse in short bursts until the mixture resembles coarse crumbs the size of peas. Stir in the pecans. Store, covered, in the refrigerator. **Yield: 2 cups**

Cream Cheese Frosting

4 ounces cream cheese,
    softened
1 tablespoon unsalted butter,
    softened
1/2 teaspoon vanilla extract
1 drop of orange extract
1 1/2 cups sifted confectioners'
    sugar
2 tablespoons heavy whipping
    cream

Beat the cream cheese and butter in a mixer bowl until creamy. Add vanilla and orange extracts and mix well. Add confectioners' sugar gradually, beating constantly for 5 minutes. Beat in whipping cream until blended. **Yield: 2 cups**

There ain't nothing more country than freshly made fried pies!

Company's Comin' Fried Pies

Pie Dough
2 teaspoons powdered milk
$^1/_3$ cup lukewarm water
$^3/_4$ cup lard
1 egg, beaten
3 cups flour
$^1/_4$ teaspoon baking powder
1 teaspoon salt

Filling
2 cups diced apricots,
 peaches or apples
$^1/_2$ cup packed light brown sugar
2 tablespoons unsalted butter
$^1/_4$ teaspoon cinnamon
$^1/_8$ teaspoon salt
Shortening for frying

Mix milk powder with warm water in a medium bowl. Cut lard into milk mixture until slightly dissolved and stir in beaten egg. Mix the flour, baking powder and salt. Add flour mixture gradually into milk mixture, stirring constantly. Cover and refrigerate for 2 hours or longer, best when refrigerated overnight. For the filling, chop the fruit into thumb-sized pieces and place in heavy saucepan. Cover the fruit with water and bring to a boil; reduce heat. Simmer until fruit absorbs the water and becomes "jam like," about 25 to 30 minutes. Remove from heat and mash the brown sugar, butter, cinnamon and salt into fruit until it becomes like a thick chunky jam. Divide the dough into 10 little balls and roll out between waxed paper into 6-inch circles. Place 2 tablespoons of the filling into the middle of each and fold over pastry into half moon shapes. Rub a little water on edges so the pastry sticks together then mash firmly with a fork to tightly seal. If you don't seal the edges properly the filling will run out. Melt enough shortening in a heavy skillet to make $^3/_4$-inch depth. Oil should be about 350 degrees. Fry pies 1 at a time until golden brown. Cool on a wire rack over a metal baking sheet. Sprinkle with granulated sugar, confectioners' sugar or sugar glaze. Best eaten while still warm. **Yield: 10 fried pies**

These tasty treats will last several days.
The apricot ones are my favorites.

Old-Fashioned Meat Loaf

Meat Loaf

- 4 pounds ground beef or ground turkey
- 2 cups crumbled-up biscuits
- 1 cup Ritz cracker crumbs
- 1 cup finely chopped onion
- 2/3 cup finely chopped green bell pepper
- 1/2 cup finely grated carrot
- 1/2 cup heavy whipping cream
- 3 eggs, beaten
- 2 tablespoons Famous Dave's BBQ sauce
- 1 tablespoon Famous Dave's Steak seasoning
- 2 teaspoons Famous Dave's Georgia Mustard sauce

Topping

- 1 cup catsup
- 1/4 cup packed light brown sugar
- 2 tablespoons finely chopped onion
- 2 tablespoons finely chopped green bell pepper

For the meat loaf, combine ground beef, biscuit crumbs, cracker crumbs, onion, green pepper, carrot, cream, eggs, BBQ sauce, steak seasoning and mustard sauce in a bowl and mix well. Shape the ground beef mixture into 2 loaves. Place each loaf in a greased 5x9-inch loaf pan. Preheat the oven to 350 degrees.

For the topping, combine catsup, brown sugar, onion and green pepper in a saucepan. Simmer until the vegetables are tender, stirring occasionally. Pour over the loaves. Bake for 1 hour. Using biscuits instead of bread is just an excuse to whip up a batch! **Yield: 12 servings**

This is the best meat loaf you'll ever eat, and I don't care who your grandmother is!

Twice-Smoked Orgasmic Ham

1 (12- to 15-pound) smoked bone-in ham
Whole cloves
Pineapple slices
Maraschino cherries
1 cup frozen tangerine juice concentrate
1 cup Polaner apricot preserves

1/2 cup French Pommery mustard
1/2 cup Grey Poupon Dijon mustard
1 cup packed light brown sugar
1 teaspoon ground cloves
1/2 teaspoon coarse ground black pepper
1/2 teaspoon cayenne

To make this ham, I use the indirect method of slow-cooking as described on page 13, so get your covered charcoal grill ready! Score the ham in a cross diamond pattern. Stud the ham with whole cloves at each intersection. Smoke at 225 degrees for 3 hours. Remove the ham and place on sheet pan. Secure the pineapple slices and the cherries to the ham with toothpicks. To make the glaze, combine the tangerine juice concentrate, preserves, mustards, brown sugar, ground cloves and peppers in a bowl and mix well. Generously slather the ham with glaze and bake in a 350-degree oven for 1 1/2 hours. Brush the ham with glaze every 20 minutes. Remove from the oven and let rest for 30 minutes before carving. This ham is soo good it will have you Oooing and Ahhing!

Yield: 10 to 12 servings

Famous Dave's Corn Bread with Jalapeño Honey Glaze

1 cup yellow cornmeal
1 cup stone-ground cornmeal
1 (9-ounce) package yellow cake mix
2 teaspoons baking powder
1 teaspoon salt
1/8 teaspoon cayenne
1/2 cup milk
1/2 cup buttermilk
1/4 cup vegetable oil
2 eggs, beaten
2 tablespoons light brown sugar
2 tablespoons honey
1 tablespoon mayonnaise
Jalapeño Honey Glaze

Mix yellow cornmeal, stone-ground cornmeal, cake mix, baking powder, salt and cayenne in a bowl. Combine milk, buttermilk, oil, eggs, brown sugar and honey in a bowl and mix well. Add to the cornmeal mixture and mix gently; there should be no lumps, but do not over mix. Fold in the mayonnaise. Let rest, covered, in the refrigerator for 30 minutes or up to overnight. Preheat the oven to 400 degrees. Spoon the cold batter into a muffin tin or cast-iron skillet. Bake for 25 to 30 minutes or until a knife inserted in the center comes out clean and the top is golden brown. Drizzle the warm corn bread with Jalapeño Honey Glaze.

Yield: 9 servings

Jalapeño Honey Glaze

1/2 cup butter
1 large jalapeño (1/8-inch pieces), seeded
3 tablespoons (1/8-inch pieces) red bell pepper
1/4 cup honey
1/8 teaspoon cayenne

Heat butter in a saucepan until melted. Stir in jalapeño and red pepper. Bring to a simmer. Stir in honey and cayenne. Bring to a simmer, stirring occasionally. Remove from heat. Store, covered, in the refrigerator. Reheat before serving. Drizzle over Famous Dave's Corn Bread.

Yield: 1/4 cup

In my succotash recipe I use baby lima beans because they are more flavorful and tender.

Indian Succotash

4 cups sweet corn niblets
1 (14½-ounce) can chicken broth
2 cups baby lima beans
½ cup chopped onion
½ cup chopped red bell pepper
½ cup chopped green bell pepper

2 ounces chopped salt pork
½ teaspoon coarse ground black pepper
¼ teaspoon salt
¼ teaspoon cayenne
¼ cup butter
¾ cup heavy whipping cream

Combine the corn, broth, lima beans, onion, red pepper, green pepper, salt pork, black pepper, salt and cayenne in a large saucepan. Bring to a boil; reduce heat. Simmer for 10 minutes, stirring occasionally. Drain, reserving the broth. Add the salt pork back to the broth. Bring the broth and salt pork to a boil in a saucepan. Boil until reduced to ½ cup. Add the butter, stirring until melted. Return the vegetables to the saucepan. Cook until heated through, stirring occasionally. Remove from heat. Stir in the whipping cream. Serve immediately. **Yield: 4 to 6 servings**

Fire and Ice Cukes & Onions

2 medium cucumbers
1 medium white onion
1 cup vinegar
1 cup sugar
1 cup water

¼ teaspoon coarse ground black pepper
¼ teaspoon crushed red pepper flakes
¼ teaspoon celery seeds
1 teaspoon salt
¼ teaspoon cayenne

Slice cucumbers and onion on a French mandolin with the grate or waffle edge ⅛ inch thick. Place in bowl. Mix vinegar, sugar, water, black pepper, red pepper flakes, celery seeds, salt and cayenne in a bowl, making sure the sugar is dissolved. Pour over cucumbers and onion. Separate onion and toss cucumbers to thoroughly coat with the marinade. Chill in refrigerator overnight. To serve, drain and reserve marinade, which can be used again. **Yield: 4 to 6 servings**

Big Mama's Spanish Rice

¹/₄ cup butter
1 cup uncooked long grain white rice
1 tablespoon Famous Dave's BBQ sauce
1 teaspoon Famous Dave's Steak seasoning
1 teaspoon chili powder
¹/₂ teaspoon red pepper sauce
¹/₄ teaspoon cumin
¹/₈ teaspoon cayenne

¹/₄ teaspoon garlic powder
¹/₂ cup finely chopped onion
¹/₄ cup finely chopped green bell pepper
1 jalapeño, finely diced
1 (16-ounce) can diced and peeled
  tomatoes
1 (14¹/₂-ounce) can chicken broth

In a large skillet melt the butter and sauté rice until lightly browned. Add BBQ sauce, seasonings, onion, green pepper, and jalapeño and cook until tender but not brown, stirring frequently. Add tomatoes and chicken broth and bring to a boil. Cover and simmer for 20 minutes. Remove from heat, mix up and serve. **Yield: 4 to 6 servings**

Heavenly Deviled Eggs

12 eggs
4 ounces cream cheese, softened
¼ cup mayonnaise-type salad dressing
3 tablespoons sweet pickle relish
1 tablespoon finely chopped pimento
1 tablespoon Famous Dave's BBQ sauce
2 teaspoons Famous Dave's Georgia Mustard sauce
1 teaspoon Famous Dave's Steak seasoning
½ teaspoon ground white pepper
    Paprika to taste

Pierce a small hole in the large end of each egg to center the yolk. Place the eggs in a large saucepan. Add enough cold water to cover. Bring to a boil. Remove from heat and cover. Let stand for 20 minutes; drain. Add cold water to cover. Repeat the draining and covering with cold water process several times or until the eggs are cool. Bang the eggs together under running water to loosen the eggs from the shells. Discard shells and drain eggs. Cut the eggs lengthwise into halves. Remove the yolks and arrange the egg whites on a serving platter. Rinse egg whites if necessary and pat dry. Mash the egg yolks in a bowl. Add the cream cheese, salad dressing, pickle relish, pimento, BBQ sauce, mustard sauce, steak seasoning and white pepper and mix well. Spoon the yolk mixture into a pastry bag. Pipe into the egg whites. Sprinkle with paprika. Chill, covered, until serving time. **Yield: 24 servings**

For fun be creative with your egg garnishes. Try little shrimp, black olives, sweet pickles, smoked salmon, or pimento strips.

Southern Charm Sweet Potato Casserole

3 pounds sweet potatoes, peeled
1/2 cup packed light brown sugar
1/2 cup unsalted butter
2 tablespoons frozen tangerine
   juice concentrate
1 tablespoon Amaretto
1 tablespoon Kahlúa

1/2 teaspoon salt
1/2 teaspoon cinnamon
1 teaspoon vanilla
   extract
2 lightly beaten eggs
1/4 cup toasted pecans
Large marshmallows

Cube sweet potatoes and combine with enough cold water to cover in saucepan. Bring to a boil; reduce heat. Simmer for 30 minutes or until tender; drain. Mash with a potato masher. Spoon the mashed sweet potatoes into a mixer bowl. Beat until blended. Add brown sugar, butter, tangerine juice concentrate, Amaretto, Kahlúa, salt, cinnamon and vanilla. Beat until smooth. Add the eggs, beating until blended. Stir in the pecans. Spoon the sweet potato mixture into a buttered 2-quart baking dish. Bake at 350 degrees for 20 minutes. Top with marshmallows. Bake until marshmallows are golden brown and slightly melted. **Yield: 6 to 8 servings**

Fell-Off-The-Wagon Apples

1/2 cup chopped pecans
1 teaspoon butter
1/4 cup honey
1/4 cup packed light brown sugar
1/4 cup unsalted butter
1/4 cup tangerine juice cocktail
   concentrate or orange juice concentrate
2 tablespoons Amaretto
2 tablespoons peach schnapps

1 teaspoon vanilla extract
2 teaspoons fresh lemon juice
1 teaspoon cinnamon
1/4 teaspoon ground nutmeg
1/2 teaspoon salt
2 tablespoons cornstarch
1/2 cup water
2 pounds Granny Smith apples,
   peeled, cut into bite-size pieces

Preheat the oven to 350 degrees. Mix pecans and butter in a shallow baking dish. Toast for 13 minutes, stirring occasionally. Let stand until cool. Mix honey, brown sugar, unsalted butter and tangerine juice concentrate in a saucepan. Bring to a simmer over medium heat, stirring frequently. Stir in Amaretto, peach schnapps, vanilla, lemon juice, cinnamon, nutmeg and salt. Bring just to a boil, stirring frequently. Add a mixture of cornstarch and water. Bring to a boil. Cook until thickened, stirring constantly. Pour over the apples and toasted pecans in a bowl and toss until coated. Serve warm over ice cream. The flavor is enhanced if prepared 1 day in advance, stored covered in the refrigerator and reheated just before serving. **Yield: 6 to 8 servings**

Banana Pudding

1³/₄ cups sugar
¹/₃ cup flour
¹/₄ cup cornstarch
¹/₄ teaspoon salt
3 cups half-and-half
1 cup heavy whipping cream
6 egg yolks

¹/₄ cup melted unsalted butter
1¹/₂ teaspoons vanilla extract
1 teaspoon almond extract
1 teaspoon banana extract
1 (12-ounce) package vanilla wafers
6 medium bananas, sliced
Perfect Meringue (page 122)

Mix sugar, flour, cornstarch and salt in a saucepan. Whisk half-and-half, whipping cream, egg yolks and butter in a bowl until blended. Stir into flour mixture. Cook over medium heat just until the mixture begins to thicken, stirring constantly. Remove from heat. Stir in flavorings. Line a 3-quart baking dish with vanilla wafers. Layer half the bananas and half the custard over the wafers. Repeat the layers with the remaining vanilla wafers, remaining bananas and remaining custard. Spread the meringue over pudding, sealing to edge. Bake in 375-degree oven until meringue turns golden brown, about 15 minutes. **Yield: 8 servings**

Rice Pudding
with Drunk Raisins

*This rich, creamy, melt-in-your-mouth rice pudding
is the ultimate comfort food dessert.*

1/4 cup golden raisins
Amaretto
2/3 cup long grain converted rice
2 cups milk
1/2 cup plus 1 teaspoon sugar
1 vanilla bean
2 cups half-and-half

1 cup heavy whipping cream
3 eggs, beaten
1 teaspoon salt
1 1/4 teaspoons vanilla extract
3/4 teaspoon almond extract
Cinnamon to taste
Ground nutmeg to taste

Combine the raisins with enough Amaretto to cover in a bowl. Let stand, covered, at room temperature for 2 days. Rinse the rice and drain. Heat milk in a saucepan until bubbles form around the edge of the pan. Stir in rice. Simmer, covered, over low heat for 20 minutes. Remove from heat. Let stand until cool. Place sugar in food processor and scrape vanilla bean seeds into sugar. Discard pod or save. Process until powdery. Combine sugar mixture, raisins, half-and-half, whipping cream, eggs, salt and flavorings in a bowl and mix well. Stir in rice. Spoon into a buttered baking dish. Place dish in a larger baking pan. Add enough water to larger pan to measure 2 inches for water bath. Bake at 325 degrees for 1 hour or until golden brown, stirring every 20 minutes. Remove from water bath. Sprinkle with cinnamon and nutmeg. Let stand for 1 hour. Top with whipped cream.

Yield: 6 servings

Good Ol'-Fashioned Coconut Cake

1 cup buttermilk
2 egg yolks
1 teaspoon vanilla extract
$1/2$ teaspoon almond extract
3 cups sifted cake flour
4 teaspoons baking powder

2 cups superfine sugar
1 teaspoon salt
$3/4$ cup unsalted butter, softened
4 large egg whites
$1/4$ cup flaked fresh coconut

Lightly mix buttermilk, egg yolks, vanilla and almond extract in a medium bowl. In a large mixing bowl, combine cake flour, baking powder, sugar and salt. Mix butter into flour mixture and gradually beat in half the buttermilk mixture at low speed. Once thoroughly moistened, increase speed to medium and beat for 2 minutes. Scrape down bowl and add remaining buttermilk mixture and beat for another 2 minutes. In a medium bowl, using an electric mixer, beat egg whites to form soft peaks. Gently fold into cake batter. Add coconut and gently fold in. Pour batter into three 8-inch buttered pans that have been dusted with flour. Bake at 350 degrees for 25 to 35 minutes or until toothpick inserted in the center of the cake comes out clean. Cool layers on wire racks for 10 minutes. Loosen sides of layers with knife and remove from pans. Cool completely on wire racks before frosting.

Yield: 8 servings

Fluffy Sweet Stuff

Filling
1$1/2$ cups apricot preserves

Buttercream Frosting
8 ounces cream cheese
$3/4$ cup unsalted butter,
    softened
6 cups confectioners' sugar

Coconut Icing
4 egg whites
$2/3$ cup light corn syrup
1$1/2$ cups sugar
6 tablespoons water
2 teaspoons vanilla extract
$1/4$ teaspoon almond extract
Flaked fresh coconut

Spread each cake layer with $1/2$ cup apricot preserves. To make buttercream frosting, place cream cheese and butter in a medium bowl and beat until creamy using an electric mixer. Slowly mix in confectioners' sugar. Divide mixture in half and spread between layers; assemble coconut cake. To make coconut icing, beat egg whites in a large mixing bowl with an electric mixer until soft peaks form. Combine corn syrup, sugar and water in a medium saucepan, cover and bring to a boil. Cook over medium heat for 5 minutes. Do not burn the syrup mixture! Slowly drizzle hot syrup mixture into egg whites while beating constantly. Continue to beat until icing is glossy and forms stiff peaks. Add vanilla extract and almond extract and beat to mix. Ice cake immediately to prevent icing from hardening and gently press coconut over top and side of cake.

Black-as-Sin Espresso Chocolate Cake

2 cups flour, sifted
1³/4 cups plus 1 tablespoon sugar
2 tablespoons instant espresso powder
1 teaspoon baking soda
1 teaspoon salt
¹/2 teaspoon baking powder
³/4 cup baking cocoa
1 cup (8 ounces) hot brewed espresso

2 teaspoons vanilla extract
¹/2 teaspoon almond extract
¹/3 cup buttermilk
¹/3 cup mayonnaise
2 egg yolks, lightly beaten
¹/4 cup canola oil
³/4 cup unsalted butter, softened
Chocolate Buttercream Frosting

Mix flour, sugar, espresso powder, baking soda, salt and baking powder in a bowl. Dissolve baking cocoa in fresh brewed espresso in a bowl and mix well. Stir in flavorings. Whisk buttermilk, mayonnaise, egg yolks and canola oil in a bowl. Stir in baking cocoa mixture. Combine ¹/2 cup of the buttermilk mixture and butter in a mixer bowl and mix well. Add flour mixture. Beat at low speed just until moistened, scraping bowl occasionally. Beat at medium to high speed for 1¹/2 minutes. Add the remaining buttermilk mixture ¹/3 at a time, beating for 20 seconds after each addition and scraping the bowl occasionally. Preheat the oven to 350 degrees. Spoon the batter into 2 buttered and floured square cake pans. Bake for 40 to 45 minutes or until a wooden pick inserted in the center comes out clean. Cool in pans on a wire rack for 10 minutes. Invert onto a wire rack to cool completely. Spread Chocolate Buttercream Frosting between the layers and over the top and sides of the cake.
Yield: 8 to 10 servings

If you don't have an espresso machine, you can buy instant espresso to mix yourself or stop by your favorite coffee shop and buy it brewed.

Chocolate Buttercream Frosting

8 ounces semisweet chocolate
¹/3 cup unsalted butter
8 ounces cream cheese, softened
4 ounces heavy whipping cream
2 teaspoons instant espresso powder

1¹/2 teaspoons vanilla extract
¹/4 teaspoon almond extract
¹/2 teaspoon salt
4¹/2 cups confectioners' sugar

Heat chocolate and butter in a double boiler over low heat until melted and blended, stirring constantly. Remove from heat. Combine cream cheese and whipping cream in a mixer bowl. Beat at medium speed until smooth, scraping the bowl occasionally. Stir the espresso, flavorings and salt into chocolate mixture. Add chocolate mixture to the cream cheese mixture, beating until blended. Add confectioners' sugar gradually, beating constantly for 5 minutes or until of spreading consistency.
Yield: 2 cups

The Chicken Shack

Secret Fried Chicken Marinade

1 gallon plus 2 cups cold water
6 tablespoons chicken base
2 tablespoons salt
2 teaspoons fine ground black pepper
1 teaspoon cayenne
1 tablespoon liquid hickory smoke

Prepare 2 days before frying chicken. Bring 2 cups of water to a boil. Add chicken base and dry ingredients. Mix well and remove from heat. Add hickory smoke and immediately add to 1 gallon water. Let marinade stand overnight before using. **Yield: 1 gallon**

Real Honest Southern Fried Chicken

2 (3-pound) chickens
1 gallon Secret Fried Chicken Marinade
5 cups flour
5 tablespoons Famous Dave's
    Steak seasoning
1 tablespoon black pepper

2 teaspoons salt
1 teaspoon paprika
1/2 teaspoon cayenne
8 cups cold water
Peanut oil for frying
1/2 cup butter

The night before serving, cut chicken up; rinse. Pour the marinade over the chicken in a large bowl, turning to coat. Marinate, covered, in the refrigerator for 8 hours—no more, no less; drain. Rinse the chicken and refrigerate until ready to fry. Mix flour, steak seasoning, black pepper, salt, paprika and cayenne in a bowl. Add chicken to flour mixture. Knock the chicken together to shake off the excess flour. Dunk in the cold water and shake. Return chicken to flour mixture. This begins a series of lifting the chicken out of the flour mixture and letting it fall back. Do this about 5 times, tapping chicken pieces together several times to knock off the excess flour. Add enough peanut oil to a heavy skillet to measure 3/4 inch. Add the butter. Heat the mixture to 350 degrees. Fry chicken in the hot peanut oil for 15 minutes or until golden brown, turning the chicken frequently. Pay close attention to the temperature of the oil as the addition of the cold chicken will cool the oil. Adjust the temperature as needed. This seems like a lot of work but you'll be rewarded with the best fried chicken you've ever tasted. Your friends will want your recipe! **Yield: 4 servings**

Real good Southern Fried Chicken is definitely an art. There are no shortcuts and it sure ain't meant for folks on a diet. This recipe is the best there is—you'll never see it in another cookbook!

Ol' Southern Silky Smooth Buttermilk Biscuits

4 cups flour
2 tablespoons baking powder
2 teaspoons salt
2 teaspoons sugar
1 teaspoon baking soda

$^1/_3$ cup melted bacon grease
$^1/_4$ cup unsalted butter
$1^3/_4$ cups buttermilk
Melted unsalted butter

Mix the flour, baking powder, salt, sugar and baking soda in a bowl. Cut in the bacon grease and $^1/_4$ cup butter until the mixture resembles coarse crumbs. Add buttermilk, stirring with a fork until a soft dough forms. Knead on lightly floured surface for 10 to 20 seconds or until the dough adheres; do not overwork or the dough will be tough. Preheat oven to 450 degrees. Coat fingers lightly with additional bacon drippings. Shape the dough into 2- or 3-inch balls. Arrange the biscuits with sides touching in ungreased pans. Flatten tops slightly and lightly brush with additional bacon drippings. Bake for 12 to 15 minutes or until golden brown. Brush lightly with melted butter. Cool slightly before serving. **Yield: 12 servings**

Chicken Pan Gravy

3 tablespoons fried chicken pan drippings
$^1/_4$ cup flour
$1^1/_2$ cups chicken stock
1 cup milk
$^1/_2$ teaspoon salt
$^1/_4$ teaspoon ground black pepper
$^1/_8$ teaspoon cayenne
$^1/_8$ teaspoon ground nutmeg

Heat the pan drippings in a skillet. Stir in the flour. Cook over medium heat until light brown in color, stirring constantly. Stir in chicken stock gradually. Add milk gradually, stirring constantly until blended. Stir in salt, black pepper, cayenne and nutmeg. Simmer over low heat until thickened, stirring constantly. Serve over chicken, mashed potatoes and hot biscuits. **Yield: 2 cups**

You must make gravy. It would be a sin to waste such good drippings, and don't rush it; the longer gravy simmers the better it gets.

Southern Greens with Pot Likker

1 pound fresh spinach
1 pound fresh turnip greens
1 pound fresh mustard greens
1 pound fresh collard greens
3 large ham hocks
1 pound thick-slice hickory-smoked bacon,
  cut into 1-inch pieces
1 medium white onion, chopped

2 tablespoons cider vinegar
1 tablespoon Famous Dave's Steak seasoning
2 teaspoons red pepper sauce
2 teaspoons prepared horseradish
1 teaspoon crushed red pepper flakes
1/2 teaspoon dry mustard
Hard-boiled eggs, sliced
Chopped white onion to taste

Rinse the fresh greens several times. Discard stems and any limp, wilted or blemished leaves. Tear the greens into bite-size pieces. Combine the ham hocks with enough water to cover in a stockpot. Bring to a boil; reduce heat. Simmer, covered, for 2 hours or until the ham hocks are tender. Add the greens and additional water as needed. Fry the bacon in a skillet until crisp. Drain, reserving the bacon drippings. Crunch the bacon. Set aside. Sauté 1 onion in the reserved bacon drippings until tender. Add to the greens and mix well. Stir in the vinegar, steak seasoning, red pepper sauce, horseradish, red pepper flakes and dry mustard. Cook the greens until tender; do not overcook. Drain the greens, reserving the "pot likker." Spoon the greens into a serving bowl. Garnish with sliced hard-boiled eggs. Serve with bowls of crumbled bacon and chopped white onion and a gravy boat of "pot likker." Be sure to provide a vinegar cruet and hot sauce for the table. If fresh greens are not available substitute with frozen greens. **Yield: 12 servings**

This is a traditional southern holiday dish served at New Years for good luck throughout the upcoming year. Served with greens representing folding money, black-eyed peas represent coins. A real coin was placed under some lucky finder's plate for good luck.

Hoppin' John's Black-Eyed Peas

1 pound dried black-eyed peas
3 large fresh ham hocks
1 pound thick-slice hickory-smoked
  bacon, cut into 1-inch pieces
1 large white onion, chopped

2 teaspoons Famous Dave's Steak seasoning
2 teaspoons red pepper sauce
2 teaspoons Famous Dave's BBQ sauce
1/2 teaspoon crushed red pepper flakes
Hot cooked rice

Sort and rinse the peas. Combine the peas with enough water to cover in a bowl. Soak using package directions; drain. Combine ham hocks with enough water to cover in a stockpot. Bring to a boil; reduce heat. Simmer for 45 minutes; skim fat. Cook bacon in a large Dutch oven over low heat until partially cooked but not crispy. Add onion. Sauté until the onion is tender. Add peas and undrained ham hocks. Stir in steak seasoning, red pepper sauce, BBQ sauce and red pepper flakes. Bring to a boil; reduce heat. Simmer for 1 hour or until peas are tender, stirring frequently and adding additional water as needed. Serve over hot cooked rice with a side of fresh greens and a large glass of cold buttermilk with crumbled corn bread. **Yield: 16 servings**

Strawberry Shortcake

Strawberry Topping

- 2 quarts sliced fresh strawberries
- 2 cups sugar
- 2 cups strawberry daiquiri-margarita mix
- 1 cup grenadine
- 1 cup water

Shortcake

- 4 cups flour
- $1/2$ cup sugar
- 2 tablespoons baking powder
- 1 teaspoon baking soda
- 1 teaspoon salt
- $2/3$ cup unsalted butter
- $1/3$ cup shortening
- $2/3$ cup milk
- $2/3$ cup heavy whipping cream
- 2 eggs, beaten
- 1 teaspoon vanilla extract
- 1 egg
- 1 tablespoon heavy whipping cream
- $1/3$ cup turbinado raw sugar

For the topping, mix strawberries, sugar, daiquiri mix, grenadine and water in a bowl. Set aside.

For the shortcake, combine flour, $1/2$ cup sugar, baking powder, baking soda and salt in a bowl and mix well. Cut in butter and shortening until the mixture resembles coarse crumbs the size of peas; be careful not to get too small. Whisk milk, $2/3$ cup whipping cream, 2 beaten eggs and vanilla in a bowl until blended. Add to flour mixture all at one time and mix with a fork just until moistened. Add additional flour if needed if the dough appears too sticky. Knead lightly until mixture forms a ball, no more than 2 minutes or shortcake will be tough. Preheat oven to 350 degrees. Line a 9x13-inch cake pan with baking parchment. Press the shortcake dough evenly over bottom of prepared pan. Whisk 1 egg and 1 tablespoon whipping cream in a bowl. Brush the top of the shortcake generously with the egg mixture; you will not need the entire mixture. Sprinkle with $1/3$ cup raw sugar. Use all the sugar. Bake for 25 to 30 minutes or until a knife inserted in center comes out clean. Cool in pan on a wire rack. Cut into equal portions. Split each portion into halves. Spoon some of the strawberry topping over each bottom half. Top with the remaining shortcake halves and remaining strawberry topping. Serve with ice cream and whipped cream.

Yield: 10 to 12 servings

Famous Dave's Bread Pudding

Unsalted butter, softened
1 (1$^{1}/_{2}$-pound) loaf cinnamon egg bread
$^{2}/_{3}$ cup golden raisins
1$^{1}/_{2}$ cups sugar
4 cups milk
2 cups heavy whipping cream
$^{1}/_{4}$ cup vanilla extract
8 eggs, beaten
1 teaspoon cinnamon

Coat the bottom and side of a 2-inch deep baking dish heavily with butter. Tear the bread into 1-inch pieces. Mix with the raisins in a bowl. Spread the bread mixture evenly in the prepared dish, turning crust side down as this tends to burn easily. Whisk the sugar, milk, 2 cups whipping cream, vanilla, eggs and cinnamon in a bowl until blended. Pour over the bread mixture. Preheat the oven to 325 degrees. Place the baking dish in a 4-inch deep baking pan. Add water to reach halfway up side of the baking dish. Bake for 1 hour. Remove from water bath. Let stand for 20 minutes. Serve while still warm. Spoon into dessert bowls. Drizzle each serving with warm Ol' Southern Plantation Praline Sauce. Top with whipped cream and add a scoop of ice cream if desired.

Yield: 9 servings

Ol' Southern Plantation Praline Sauce

2 cups unsalted butter, cubed
1½ cups chopped pecans
3 pounds light brown sugar
1½ cups heavy whipping cream

½ teaspoon cinnamon
2½ cups sour cream
1½ teaspoons vanilla
   extract

Heat 1 cup of the butter in a large saucepan until melted. Add the pecans and mix well. Bring to a boil. Cook until the pecans begin to change color. Be careful! This mixture will foam over, so use a large saucepan. Add the remaining 1 cup butter and mix well. This will cool the pecan mixture and stop the cooking process. Remove from heat. Combine brown sugar, whipping cream and cinnamon in a saucepan and mix well. Cook over low heat until blended, stirring constantly; increase heat. Cook to 230 degrees on a candy thermometer. Stir in pecan mixture. Add sour cream and vanilla and mix well. Remove from heat. It is very important to follow the directions very carefully. It is absolutely essential to use a candy thermometer.

Yield: 4 cups

Easy as Pie

Store leftover pastry in refrigerator for up to one week.

Flaky Pie Crust

1 1/3 cups lard, softened
2/3 cup unsalted butter, softened
5 cups flour
2 tablespoons sugar

1/2 cup ice water
4 teaspoons nonfat dry milk
2 teaspoons salt

Mix lard and butter in a bowl until blended. Chill, covered, until firm. Mix flour and sugar in a bowl. Combine ice water, milk powder and salt in a bowl and mix well. Chill until ice cold. Cut the lard mixture into the flour mixture until mixture resembles coarse crumbs the size of peas. Freeze, covered, for 20 minutes. Sprinkle the water mixture over the crumb mixture, mixing constantly until blended. Knead gently until the pastry adheres. Divide the pastry into 4 portions. Shape each portion into a round disc. Chill, wrapped individually in plastic wrap, for 2 hours or up to overnight. Roll each portion of the pastry on a lightly floured surface, sprinkling the surface with additional sugar just before end of rolling process. Fit each pastry into a pie plate and flute edges. Fill as desired. To blind bake, fit each pastry into a pie plate and flute edges. Freeze for 10 minutes. Preheat the oven to 425 degrees. Line bottom of each pastry with baking parchment. Place pie weights or dried beans on parchment to prevent bubbles from forming. Bake for 12 minutes. Reduce oven temperature to 375 degrees. Remove pie weights or beans and baking parchment. Bake for 5 to 8 minutes longer or until golden brown. Flatten bubbles with bottom side of spoon if necessary. Yield: 4 single or 2 double pie crusts

Jack Frost's Pumpkin Pie

Flaky Pie Crust (page 119)
1 (15-ounce) can pumpkin
1 cup packed light brown sugar
1/4 cup premium clover honey
1 1/2 teaspoons cinnamon
1 teaspoon salt
3/4 teaspoon nutmeg

1/2 teaspoon ground ginger
1/8 teaspoon ground cloves
1/8 teaspoon mace
1 (12-ounce) can evaporated milk
3 eggs
1 teaspoon vanilla extract
Freshly whipped cream

Line a 9-inch pie plate with some of the pie crust pastry. Trim edge and flute. Combine pumpkin, brown sugar, honey, cinnamon, salt, nutmeg, ginger, cloves and mace in a mixer bowl, mixing by hand until blended. Whisk evaporated milk, eggs and vanilla in a bowl until blended. Add to pumpkin mixture. Beat at medium speed for 2 minutes. Preheat the oven to 450 degrees. Spoon the pumpkin mixture into the prepared pie plate. Bake for 10 minutes. Reduce the oven temperature to 350 degrees. Bake for 45 minutes longer or until a knife inserted in the center comes out clean. Cool on a wire rack. Serve with whipped cream. **Yield: 6 to 8 servings**

Harvest Pecan Pie

2 cups pecans, toasted in butter
1 unbaked (10-inch) pie shell
1 1/4 cups packed light brown sugar
2 tablespoons flour
1 teaspoon salt

1 1/4 cups light corn syrup
2 tablespoons molasses
1 1/2 teaspoons vanilla extract
1/4 teaspoon almond extract
5 eggs, lightly beaten

Arrange the pecans over the bottom of the pie shell. Preheat the oven to 325 degrees. Mix brown sugar, flour and salt in a bowl. Mix corn syrup, molasses and flavorings in a bowl. Add the syrup mixture and eggs to the flour mixture and mix well. Pour carefully into the prepared pie shell without disturbing the pecans. Bake for 40 to 45 minutes or until the center is set. Cool on a wire rack for 1 hour before serving. **Yield: 8 servings**

The secret to great pumpkin pie is the honey—a good premium clover honey magnifies all other flavors.

There are 4 secrets to this pie — the meringue gel, putting the meringue on piping hot filling, the lemon oil, and lots of practice. This meringue is guaranteed not to weep or shrink!

Dave's Perfect Lemon Meringue Pie

Secret Meringue Gel
1 cup cold water
2 tablespoons cornstarch
4 tablespoons sugar

Perfect Meringue
$^3/_4$ cup superfine sugar
1 tablespoon cornstarch
6 egg whites, at room temperature
$^1/_2$ teaspoon vanilla extract
1 baked Flaky pie shell, page 119

Filling
$1^3/_4$ cups sugar
$^2/_3$ cup cornstarch
1 teaspoon salt
2 cups water
6 large egg yolks, slightly beaten
3 tablespoons unsalted butter
$^1/_2$ cup fresh lemon juice
$^3/_4$ teaspoon lemon oil
$1^1/_2$ tablespoons grated lemon rind

Make meringue first but make sure that all ingredients for filling are measured and ready to go because one real secret is to put the meringue on a piping hot filling. To make gel, mix 1 cup cold water, 2 tablespoons cornstarch and 4 tablespoons sugar in a small saucepan. Cook over low heat until it forms a clear gel. To prepare sugar for meringue, thoroughly mix 1 tablespoon cornstarch with $^3/_4$ cup superfine sugar. Grind sugar and cornstarch mixture into a fine powder using an electric coffee bean grinder and set aside. Whip egg whites until soft peaks form. Slowly add clear gel in small amounts and thoroughly beat in. Add superfine sugar mixture 1 tablespoon at a time and thoroughly beat in slowly. Do not be impatient. This is a slow process. Whip until stiff peaks are formed and meringue is glossy. Add vanilla and beat in. Set meringue aside.

To make filling, combine sugar, cornstarch and salt in a heavy saucepan and mix well. Add about $^1/_3$ of the water and blend well until there are no lumps. Add remaining water and blend well. Over medium-low heat, slowly bring to a boil, about 5 minutes, while constantly stirring. Mixture will turn clear. Turn heat to low and simmer for about 1 minute longer. Remove about $^1/_2$ cup of the mixture from the saucepan and quickly mix into egg yolks. Once mixed, add eggs back into hot mixture and quickly but gently mix in well. Bring back to a low boil over low heat. Remove from heat and add butter, lemon juice, lemon oil and lemon rind. Gently mix well. Immediately pour into the pie shell. While still piping hot, add meringue 1 tablespoon at a time around edge of the pie, making sure that meringue touches the pie shell all the way around the edge. Pile remaining meringue in center and spread to edge. Place in a preheated 375-degree oven for 15 minutes or until meringue starts to turn a golden brown. Cool for 1 hour before serving. **Yield: 6 to 8 servings**

Grand Marnier Raisin Pie

Flaky Pie Crust for 2-crust pie (page 119)
4 teaspoons cornstarch
1¼ cups water
1 cup packed light brown sugar
½ cup frozen tangerine juice
   or orange juice concentrate
1¼ cups golden raisins

1¼ cups dark raisins
2 tablespoons Grand Marnier
2 tablespoons fresh lemon juice
1 teaspoon cinnamon
1 egg, beaten
1 tablespoon heavy whipping cream
Turbinado raw sugar to taste

Roll half the pie pastry into a 12-inch circle on a lightly floured surface. Fit into a 9-inch pie plate; flute edge. Preheat the oven to 425 degrees. Mix the cornstarch and ¼ cup of the water in a small bowl. Combine remaining 1 cup water, brown sugar and tangerine juice concentrate in a saucepan and mix well. Stir in raisins. Bring to a simmer, stirring occasionally. Simmer over low heat until the raisins plump, stirring occasionally. Stir in cornstarch mixture. Bring to a boil. Remove from heat. Stir in Grand Marnier, lemon juice and cinnamon. Spoon into the prepared pie plate. Cut some of remaining pastry into strips. Weave lattice-fashion over the pie. Brush the pastry with a mixture of the egg and whipping cream. Sprinkle with raw sugar. Bake for 45 minutes. **Yield: 6 servings**

Mom's Apple Pie

$^2/_3$ cup packed light brown sugar
3 tablespoons flour
1 tablespoon cornstarch
1 teaspoon cinnamon
$^1/_4$ teaspoon ground nutmeg
$^1/_4$ teaspoon salt
2 pounds Granny Smith apples
1 tablespoon peach schnapps
1 tablespoon Amaretto

$^1/_2$ teaspoon vanilla extract
$^1/_2$ recipe Flaky Pie
Crust (page 119)
2 tablespoons unsalted butter
1 egg
1 tablespoon heavy whipping
cream
1 teaspoon cinnamon
$^1/_4$ cup turbinado raw sugar

Preheat oven to 425 degrees. Combine brown sugar, flour, cornstarch, cinnamon, nutmeg and salt in a bowl; mix well. Peel and slice apples. Add to brown sugar mixture; gently toss. Add schnapps, Amaretto and vanilla; gently toss. Place in 9-inch pastry-lined pie pan. Dot with butter. Top with remaining pastry, seal and flute edge. To make egg wash, combine egg and whipping cream; brush over pastry. Sprinkle with mixture of 1 teaspoon cinnamon and raw sugar. Bake for 45 minutes.

Peach Pie

County Fair Blue Ribbon Peach Pie

4 pounds ripe peaches
3/4 cup brown sugar
1 tablespoon Amaretto
1/4 cup granulated sugar
2 tablespoons cornstarch
1 tablespoon flour
1 teaspoon cinnamon
1/4 teaspoon salt

1 egg, lightly beaten
1 teaspoon vanilla extract
1 teaspoon almond extract
1/4 recipe Flaky Pie Crust (page 119)
1/2 tablespoons unsalted butter
2 egg
1 tablespoon heavy whipping cream
1/4 cup turbinado raw sugar

Peel and slice peaches. Combine with brown sugar and Amaretto in a sealable plastic bag. Chill overnight. Drain, reserving peaches and 1/2 cup of the liquid. Add mixture of granulated sugar, cornstarch, flour, cinnamon and salt to peaches and mix gently. Stir in mixture of reserved liquid, 1 egg and flavorings. Preheat oven to 350 degrees. Line a 9-inch pie pan with pastry. Spoon peach mixture into pie shell and dot with butter. Cover peach filling with lattice design pastry and seal edges. Brush with a mixture of 1 egg and whipping cream and sprinkle with raw sugar. Bake for 1 hour or until filling is bubbly.

Cabins and Lodges

My mother's side of the family were Lac Courte Oreilles Chippewa Indians living up north in God's country — the tall pines and lakes country of Hayward, Wisconsin. Going "Up North" to Grandma's was always something to look forward to. I remember Friday afternoons when my dad would get off of work early. We'd load up the family station wagon and tie down the brown Samsonite and fishing poles on the luggage racks.

One of my fondest memories of growing up is waking up in the morning at my grandmother's house. It was a little cabin with only worn curtains separating the rooms, so it was very easy to hear the clanking of the wood-fired stove as it was stoked for early-morning warmth and cooking. Escaping smoke hung lazily or drifted wispily and ghostlike throughout the house. I can so vividly remember how bright the early morning sun was beaming through the kitchen curtains. My grandmother sat next to the window wearing a forever-old droopy sweater, a Prince Albert can hanging out of one pocket and her Folger's spit can in her lap.

Percolating coffee and thick slab bacon crackling in a heavy iron skillet signaled it was time for me to go to the pump outside. There's something about inhaling crisp fresh country air and walking through grass heavy with early-morning dew, and the woodsy aroma surrounding the cabin that seems to say that everything in the world is okay. At the pump I would remove boards and reach down in the well to pull up a bucket where we kept the commodity butter, milk, and eggs. To me there ain't a better meal in the world than fresh farm eggs fried in bacon grease, hot buttered biscuits smothered with blackberry jam, and fried potatoes cooked to a golden crustiness on an old wood stove.

In the afternoons we would dig worms from the garden and, carrying our worm cans, fishing poles, and empty buckets for berry picking, we'd all walk down to the lake. We swam and fished all afternoon. I guess to my mom there wasn't anything more rewarding than watching one of her kid's wide eyes catching his first scrappy panfish as the bobber danced and darted underwater. We couldn't afford stringers so we would keep our fish on skinny tree branches stuck in the sand. A McDonald's fish fillet doesn't even come close to a freshly filleted crappie dredged in flour and cornmeal, frying in lard over an open campfire as the sun sets.

For a special treat my parents would take us to the Old Logging Camp Cook Shanty where they featured community-style dining just like in the old lumberjack days. Everything was brought to the table huge and in its entirety — whole turkeys, whole loaves of bread, big bowls of mashed potatoes, and whole pies. This made my grandmother, who used to cook for logging camps, recall how she would have to bake hundreds of pies and hundreds of loaves of bread every morning . . . or so it seemed. This section is dedicated to the generous, delicious meals of cabin and lodge kitchens.

TIMBER TRAILS

Cook Shanty Sticky Buns

Unsalted butter, softened
Ol' Southern Plantation Praline Sauce (page 115)
1 pound pecan halves
2 tablespoons yeast
$1/8$ teaspoon sugar
$1/2$ cup lukewarm water
$3/4$ cup unsalted butter, melted
$1/2$ cup sugar
$1^1/2$ cups buttermilk, heated

2 tablespoons nonfat dry milk
3 eggs, lightly beaten
2 teaspoons salt
6 cups flour
1 cup unsalted butter, softened
1 cup plus 1 tablespoon packed
 light brown sugar
$1/2$ cup heavy whipping cream
2 teaspoons cinnamon

Coat the bottom and sides of a 9x13-inch baking dish with butter. Add praline sauce to a depth of $1/4$ inch. Arrange the pecans evenly over the sauce. Dissolve the yeast and $1/8$ teaspoon sugar in the lukewarm water in a bowl and mix well. Mix $3/4$ cup melted butter and $1/2$ cup sugar in a bowl. Stir in buttermilk, milk powder, eggs, salt and yeast mixture. Add the flour and mix well. Knead on a lightly floured surface for 5 minutes. Place in a warm buttered bowl, turning to coat surface. Let rise, covered with a moist towel, in a warm place for 1 hour. Punch the dough down. Let rest for 5 minutes. Roll into a rectangle on a lightly floured surface. Spread with 1 cup softened butter. Sprinkle with a mixture of the brown sugar, whipping cream and cinnamon. Roll as for a jelly roll. Cut into $1^1/2$-inch slices. Arrange cut side up in a single layer in the prepared baking dish. Let rise in a warm place for 30 to 40 minutes. Preheat the oven to 350 degrees. Bake for 35 to 40 minutes or until light brown. Invert onto a serving platter; do not remove the baking dish for several minutes. Separate the buns and spread with additional praline sauce. You won't find a better sticky bun anywhere! **Yield: 12 large buns**

This is where it all started—
Grand Pines Lodge,
home of Famous Dave's,
Hayward, Wisconsin.

Lumberjack Camp Cinnamon Rolls

2 tablespoons dry yeast
1/8 teaspoon sugar
1/2 cup lukewarm water
3/4 cup slightly melted butter
1/2 cup sugar
1 1/2 cups buttermilk, heated
2 tablespoons nonfat dry milk powder
3 eggs, lightly beaten
2 teaspoons salt
6 cups flour
3/4 cup butter, softened
1 cup packed light brown sugar
1/4 cup cinnamon
1/2 teaspoon nutmeg
Cream Cheese Frosting

Dissolve the yeast and 1/8 teaspoon sugar in lukewarm water in a small bowl. Combine 3/4 cup melted butter and 1/2 cup sugar in a bowl and mix well. Stir in yeast mixture, buttermilk, milk powder, eggs and salt. Add flour, stirring until blended. Knead the dough on a lightly floured surface for 5 minutes. Place in a heated buttered bowl, turning to coat the surface. Let rise, covered with a damp towel, in a warm place for 1 hour. Punch the dough down. Let rest for 5 minutes. Roll the dough into a rectangle on a lightly floured surface. Spread with 3/4 cup softened butter. Sprinkle with a mixture of brown sugar, cinnamon and nutmeg. Roll as for a jelly roll. Cut into twelve 1-inch slices. Arrange the slices cut side up in a buttered 9x13-inch baking pan. Let rise in a warm place for 30 to 40 minutes. Preheat the oven to 350 degrees. Bake for 35 to 40 minutes or until light brown. Spread the warm rolls with Cream Cheese Frosting. **Yield: 12 rolls**

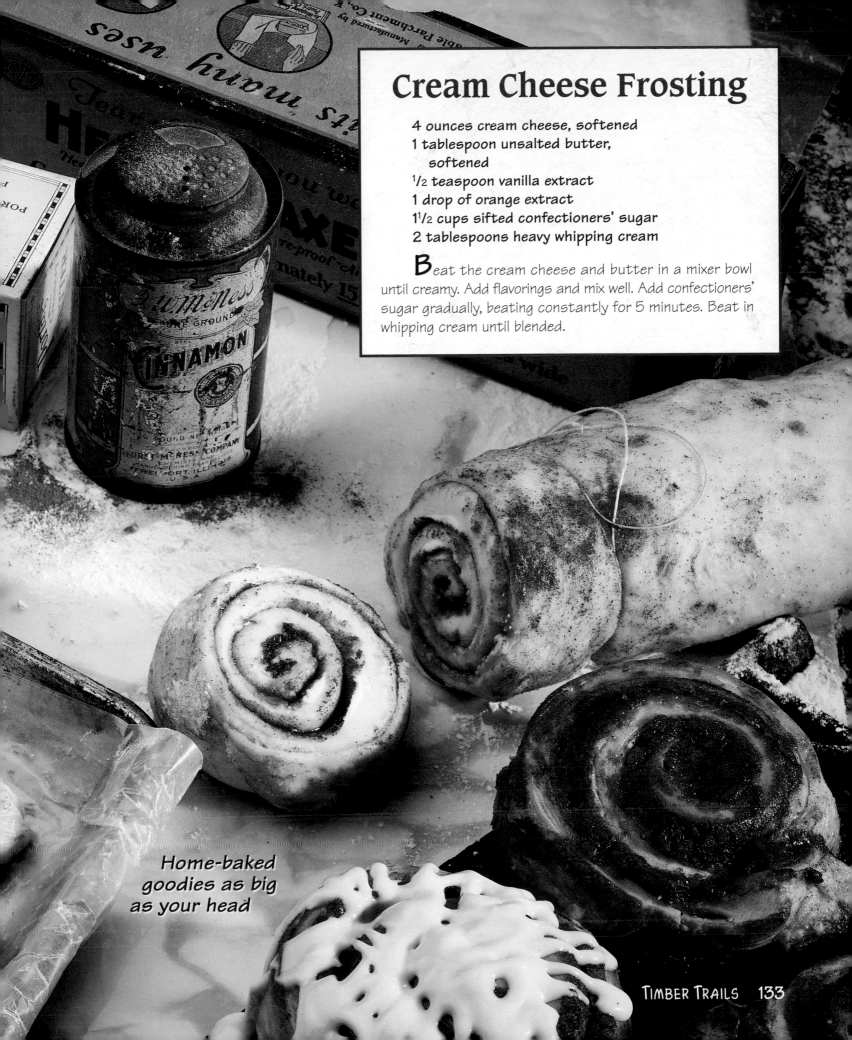

Cream Cheese Frosting

4 ounces cream cheese, softened
1 tablespoon unsalted butter,
    softened
1/2 teaspoon vanilla extract
1 drop of orange extract
1 1/2 cups sifted confectioners' sugar
2 tablespoons heavy whipping cream

Beat the cream cheese and butter in a mixer bowl until creamy. Add flavorings and mix well. Add confectioners' sugar gradually, beating constantly for 5 minutes. Beat in whipping cream until blended.

Home-baked
goodies as big
as your head

Buttermilk Clouds Blueberry Pancakes

4 cups flour
1 cup packed light brown sugar
2 tablespoons sugar
1 tablespoon baking soda
1 tablespoon baking powder
2 teaspoons salt
4 cups buttermilk
1 cup melted unsalted butter
2 teaspoons vanilla extract
1 cup whole blueberries

Mix flour, brown sugar, sugar, baking soda, baking powder and salt in a bowl. Combine buttermilk, butter and vanilla in a bowl and mix well. Stir into the flour mixture. Let stand for 20 minutes. Pour $1/4$ cup of the batter onto a hot buttered griddle for each pancake. Sprinkle with blueberries. Griddle until the edges look set and bubbles appear on the surface and pancakes turn golden brown. Serve with Blueberry Skies Syrup. **Yield: 4 servings**

Blueberry Skies Syrup

1 cup puréed blueberries
1 cup whole blueberries
1 cup Asti Spumante
2 tablespoons fresh lemon juice
$1/4$ teaspoon cinnamon
$1/4$ teaspoon vanilla extract
$1/2$ cup sugar
$1/4$ cup honey

Combine blueberry purée, blueberries, wine, lemon juice, cinnamon and vanilla in a saucepan. Bring to a boil over high heat, stirring frequently. Stir in sugar and honey. Bring to a boil. Boil for 3 minutes, stirring frequently. Store, covered, in the refrigerator. **Yield: 2 cups**

Before serving, splash with a little Harvey's Bristol Cream Sherry.

Chippewa Lakes Chicken Wild Rice Soup

1/2 cup plus 2 tablespoons butter
1 cup flour
2 tablespoons chicken fat or butter
1 cup finely chopped celery
1 cup diagonally sliced carrot
1 cup finely chopped onion
1/3 cup finely chopped green bell pepper
1/3 cup finely chopped red bell pepper
2 cups white Shoe Peg corn or corn niblets
2 cups sliced mushrooms
1 medium jalapeño
1 gallon homemade or canned chicken broth
1 tablespoon finely chopped fresh parsley
1 teaspoon salt
1/4 teaspoon black pepper
1/4 teaspoon white pepper
1/4 teaspoon ground nutmeg
1/4 teaspoon cayenne
1 1/2 pounds chicken breasts, cooked, coarsely chopped
3 cups cooked wild rice
1 cup heavy whipping cream
1/2 cup slivered almonds, toasted

Heat the butter in a skillet until hot. Stir in the flour. Cook over low heat for 2 minutes or until of the consistency of a roux, stirring constantly; do not brown. Heat the chicken fat in a large saucepan until hot. Add the celery, carrot, onion, green pepper and red pepper. Sauté until the onion is tender. Stir in corn, mushrooms and jalapeño. Cook until the mushrooms begin to turn golden brown, stirring frequently. Remove from heat. Bring broth to a boil in a 2-gallon stockpot. Stir in roux. Simmer until thickened, stirring frequently. Stir in vegetable mixture, parsley, salt, black pepper, white pepper, nutmeg and cayenne. Bring to a simmer, stirring occasionally. Add chicken, wild rice and whipping cream and mix gently. Cook just until heated through, stirring occasionally. Ladle into soup bowls. Sprinkle with the almonds.
Yield: 16 to 18 servings

Paul Bunyan's Chopper Toppers

6 large russet potatoes
2 tablespoons cooking oil
Kosher salt
6 tablespoons whipped butter
$^3/_4$ cup sour cream
3 cups beef brisket, pork shoulder or
   barbequed chicken
$^3/_4$ cup Famous Dave's BBQ sauce
$1^1/_2$ cups shredded Cheddar cheese
2 tablespoons chopped chives
6 tablespoons chopped green
   onion tops
1 green bell pepper, chopped
6 slices crisp-fried bacon, crumbled

Preheat the oven to 375 degrees. Wash and scrub the potatoes. Poke several holes in the skin. Coat with oil and generously cover with kosher salt. Bake for 45 minutes to 1 hour, depending on size of potato. Check tenderness by sticking with a fork. Cut down center of potato. Pinch in from the sides to fluff up. Stuff with whipped butter, sour cream, your choice of beef brisket, chopped pork shoulder or chicken. Slather BBQ sauce over meat. Top with shredded Cheddar cheese, chives, green onions, green pepper and bacon. **Yield: 6 servings**

Ketchikan Lodge Salmon Pâté

1 (15-ounce) can red salmon, drained
8 ounces cream cheese, softened
2 tablespoons Famous Dave's
    BBQ sauce
2 teaspoons fresh lemon juice
1 teaspoon prepared horseradish
1 teaspoon Worcestershire sauce
1/2 teaspoon salt

1/4 teaspoon white pepper
1/4 teaspoon liquid smoke
1 tablespoon finely minced onion
1 tablespoon finely minced
    seeded jalapeño
1 pimento-stuffed olive, sliced
Sliced almonds
Thinly sliced celery

Remove skin and bones from salmon and flake. Combine cream cheese, BBQ sauce, lemon juice, horseradish, Worcestershire sauce, salt, white pepper and liquid smoke in a blender container. Process until smooth. Combine the cream cheese mixture, salmon, onion and jalapeño in a bowl and mix well. Spoon into a fish mold and press lightly. Invert onto a serving platter. Arrange olive to represent eye, sliced almonds to represent fish scales and celery for the tail. Serve with Indian Maiden Fry Bread on page 140 and/or assorted party crackers. May substitute fresh smoked flaked salmon for the canned salmon. **Yield: 12 servings**

Indian Maiden Fry Bread

$1/4$ cup (115-degree) warm water
2 envelopes dry yeast
$1/2$ teaspoon sugar
$1^3/4$ cups lukewarm water
$1/4$ cup nonfat dry milk
2 tablespoons peanut oil

1 tablespoon sugar
1 teaspoon salt
6 cups flour
2 teaspoons baking powder
Peanut oil for frying

Warm a heavy ceramic cup under hot running water. Combine $1/4$ cup warm water, yeast and $1/2$ teaspoon sugar in the warm cup and mix well. Set aside. Warm a glass measuring cup under hot running water. Add $1^3/4$ cups lukewarm water, milk powder, 2 tablespoons peanut oil, 1 tablespoon sugar and salt to the warm measuring cup and mix well. Mix the flour and baking powder in a bowl. Make a well in the center of flour. Pour the yeast and milk mixtures into the well and mix gently. Knead for 6 to 8 minutes. Place the dough in an oiled bowl, turning to coat the surface. Let rise, covered with a moist towel, in a warm draft-free place for 45 minutes; do not punch the dough down. Add enough peanut oil to a large heavy skillet to measure $1/2$ inch. Heat over medium-high heat until a small piece of the dough bubbles and dances in the oil, then decrease the heat to medium. Pinch off a tennis ball-sized piece of dough and flatten while pulling at the dough to form a 6-inch disc. Do not do this on a table. Hold the dough in front of you, so when you pull gravity will help stretch the dough. Fry in the hot oil until golden brown on both sides; drain. Repeat the procedure with the remaining dough. **Yield: 12 servings**

Campfire Indian Tacos

2 pounds freshly ground beef
$1/2$ cup chopped white onion
$1/4$ cup chili powder
1 jalapeño, chopped
1 tablespoon cumin
1 tablespoon Famous Dave's Steak seasoning

1 teaspoon minced garlic
$1/2$ teaspoon coarse ground black pepper
$1/2$ teaspoon crushed red pepper flakes
$1/8$ teaspoon cayenne
Indian Maiden Fry Bread

Brown the ground beef with the onion, chili powder, jalapeño, cumin, steak seasoning, garlic, black pepper, red pepper flakes and cayenne in a large heavy skillet, stirring until the ground beef is crumbly; drain. Serve on Indian Maiden Fry Bread. Garnish with cheese, lettuce, tomatoes and onion.
Yield: 6 servings

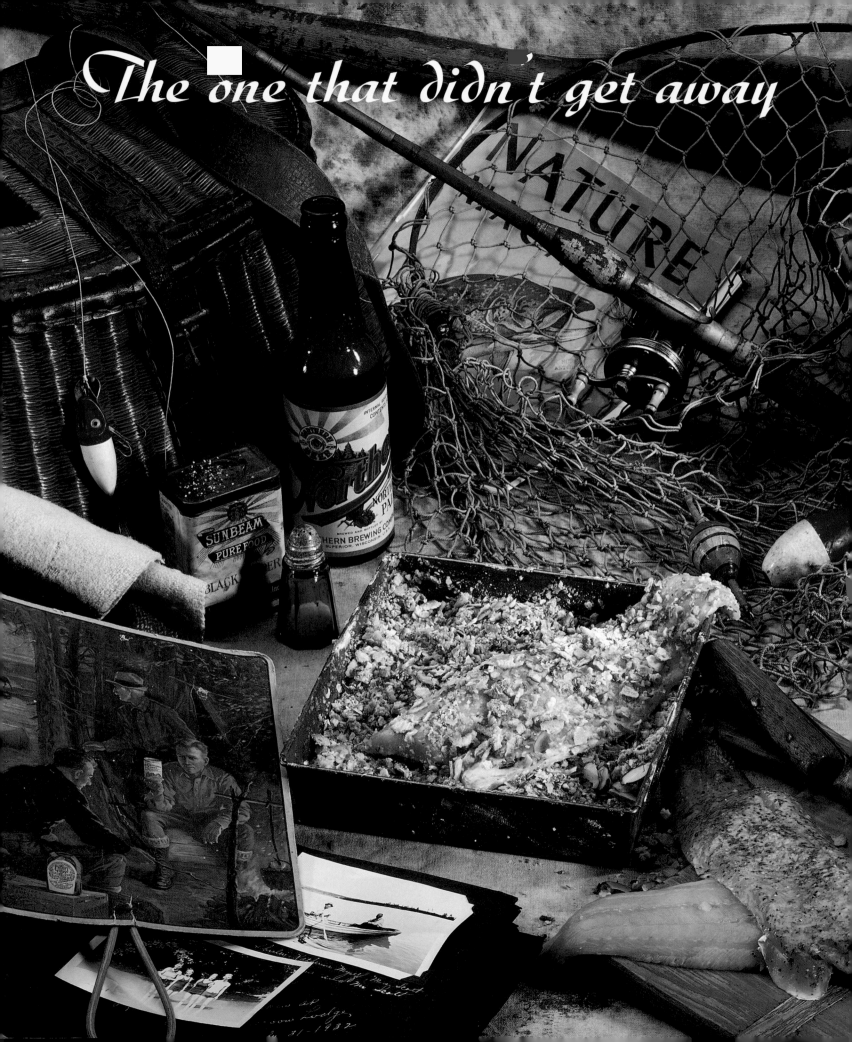

The one that didn't get away

Mom holding dinner

Sunfish Bay Shore Lunch
"Walleye Ala Ritz"

1 cup unsalted butter, softened
1 tablespoon finely chopped parsley
1 tablespoon chopped pimento
4 garlic cloves, smashed and finely diced
1 tablespoon fresh lemon juice
3 cups flour
1 tablespoon kosher salt
1 tablespoon garlic seasoning
1 teaspoon coarse ground black pepper
1/2 teaspoon cayenne
4 eggs

1/3 cup honey
1/2 cup half-and-half
2 sleeves (76) coarsely crushed Ritz crackers
1 cup crushed pecans
2 tablespoons rough chopped fresh parsley
6 (8- to 10-ounce) Walleye fillets
1/4 cup butter
1/4 cup peanut oil
3/4 cup toasted slivered almonds

To make lodge butter, mix softened butter, finely chopped parsley, chopped pimento, smashed garlic cloves and fresh lemon juice. Form into a 1 1/2-inch round log. Roll in waxed paper. Refrigerate until butter is hard. Slice into 3/8-inch slices. Make seasoned flour by combining flour, kosher salt, garlic seasoning, coarse ground black pepper and cayenne in a bowl and mixing well. Make honey milk wash by beating 4 eggs in a separate bowl and adding honey and half-and-half and mixing well. Make Ritz cracker crumb mixture by combining Ritz cracker crumbs, crushed pecans and rough chopped parsley in a third bowl. Prepare fillets by dipping them into seasoned flour. Shake off excess. Dip in honey milk wash. Dip in Ritz cracker crumb mixture. Melt 1/4 cup butter in a large fry pan and add peanut oil. When hot, sauté fillets until they turn golden brown. The fish will not be done. Finish cooking in a preheated 350-degree oven for 10 to 15 minutes or until the fillets flake. After removing from oven, place lodge butter slice on each fillet and garnish with 2 tablespoons of the toasted almond slivers. Serve immediately. **Yield: 6 servings**

Cheddar Corn Bread Topping

2 cups stone-ground
   cornmeal
1 cup yellow cornmeal
1 (9-ounce) package yellow
   cake mix
$1/2$ cup flour
2 tablespoons light
   brown sugar
2 tablespoons sugar
1 tablespoon baking powder
1 teaspoon salt
$1/2$ cup milk
$1/2$ cup buttermilk
$1/4$ cup bacon drippings
2 eggs, beaten
1 cup shredded Cheddar
   cheese
1 red jalapeño, finely minced

Mix stone-ground cornmeal,
yellow cornmeal, cake mix, flour, brown
sugar, sugar, baking powder and salt
in a bowl. Whisk the milk, buttermilk,
bacon drippings and eggs in a bowl.
Stir in the cheese and jalapeño. Add
to the cornmeal mixture and mix well;
batter should not be lumpy, but do
not over mix. Let the batter rest,
covered, in the refrigerator for 30
minutes or up to overnight for best
results. Spoon batter on chicken
pot pie mixture and bake according
to chicken pot pie directions.
Yield: 9 servings

Log Cabin Chicken Pot Pie

1/2 recipe Flaky Pie Crust (page 119)
6 tablespoons butter
3/4 cup flour
4 cups chicken stock
1/2 cup heavy whipping cream
1/2 teaspoon ground nutmeg
1/4 teaspoon rubbed thyme
1/4 teaspoon coarse ground pepper
1/4 teaspoon toasted sesame seed oil
2/3 cup torn mushrooms
2/3 cup baby sweet niblet corn
1/2 cup (1/2-inch pieces) slender asparagus

1/2 cup chopped red potatoes
1/2 cup frozen pearl onions
1/2 cup finely chopped celery
1/3 cup diagonally sliced carrot
1/3 cup baby green peas
2 tablespoons minced fresh parsley
2 tablespoons slivered almonds, toasted
2 teaspoons finely chopped jalapeño
1 teaspoon Famous Dave's Steak seasoning
3 cups chopped cooked chicken
1 recipe uncooked Cheddar Corn Bread

Line the bottom and sides of a 9x13-inch glass or ceramic baking dish with the pie crust pastry. Heat the butter in a large heavy saucepan until melted. Add the flour gradually, stirring constantly until blended. Cook over low heat for 2 minutes or until of a roux consistency; do not brown. Add the stock gradually, whisking constantly until blended. Stir in the whipping cream, nutmeg, thyme, pepper and sesame seed oil. Add the mushrooms, corn, asparagus, red potatoes, pearl onions, celery, carrot, peas, parsley, almonds, jalapeño and steak seasoning and mix well. Simmer for 20 minutes, stirring occasionally. Add the chicken carefully and mix gently. Preheat the oven to 400 degrees. Spoon the chicken mixture into the pastry-lined dish. Spread with the Cheddar Corn Bread batter. Bake for 45 to 50 minutes or until a wooden pick inserted in the center comes out clean. Let stand for several minutes before serving. **Yield: 9 servings**

Buttermilk Yeast Rolls

1 tablespoon yeast
¹/₄ teaspoon sugar
¹/₄ cup lukewarm water
¹/₂ cup buttermilk
¹/₄ cup half-and-half
3 tablespoons sugar

2 tablespoons plus 1 teaspoon
  nonfat dry milk
2¹/₂ teaspoons salt
2 eggs, lightly beaten
3¹/₂ cups flour
¹/₄ cup unsalted butter, melted

Dissolve yeast and ¹/₄ teaspoon sugar in lukewarm water in a small bowl. Combine buttermilk, half-and-half, 3 tablespoons sugar, milk powder, salt and eggs in a bowl and mix well. Stir in yeast mixture. Add 1¹/₂ cups of the flour and mix until smooth. Add the remaining 2 cups flour and mix well. Knead on a lightly floured surface for 5 minutes. Shape into a ball. Place in a buttered bowl, turning to coat the surface. Let rise, covered, until doubled in bulk. Punch the dough down. Let rest for 5 minutes. Shape the dough into 2-inch balls. Arrange in a greased 9x13-inch baking pan. Cover with buttered plastic wrap; cover with a towel. Let rise for 45 minutes. Preheat the oven to 350 degrees. Bake for 30 to 40 minutes or until golden brown. Brush tops of rolls with butter. Serve rolls immediately.

Yield: 12 servings

After Church Country Roast Chicken

Roast Chicken Seasoning
$1/2$ cup kosher salt
$1/2$ cup paprika
$1/2$ cup lemon pepper
$1/2$ cup Mrs. Dash original blend

Roast Chicken
1 (6-pound) roasting chicken
2 (16-ounce) bottles Italian dressing
1 (8-ounce) bottle lemon juice
$1/3$ cup Roast Chicken Seasoning

Mix ingredients for chicken seasoning. Store in a covered container. Place the chicken in a 2-gallon sealable plastic bag. Pour a mixture of the Italian dressing and lemon juice over chicken, turning to coat. Marinate in refrigerator for 3 hours, turning every 30 minutes. Remove chicken from bag and drain. Season generously with $1/3$ cup Roast Chicken Seasoning. Preheat the oven to 375 degrees. Arrange chicken on a rack in a baking pan. Tent loosely with foil. Bake for $1^1/2$ to 2 hours or until a meat thermometer registers 170 to 180 degrees, removing the tent 20 minutes before the end of the baking process. Let stand for 10 minutes before carving.

Yield: 6 to 8 main dish servings and 2 cups seasoning

Buttermilk Banana Bread

1 1/2 cups all-purpose flour
1 cup whole wheat flour
1/2 cup packed light brown sugar
1/2 cup sugar
1 1/2 teaspoons salt
1 teaspoon baking powder
1 teaspoon baking soda
1 teaspoon cinnamon

1/4 teaspoon ground nutmeg
3 cups very ripe mashed bananas
  (about 6 bananas)
1/2 cup buttermilk
1/2 cup unsalted butter, softened
1/4 cup honey
2 eggs, lightly beaten
1/2 teaspoon banana extract

Mix all-purpose flour, whole wheat flour, brown sugar, sugar, salt, baking powder, baking soda, cinnamon and nutmeg in a bowl. Combine bananas, buttermilk, butter, honey, eggs and flavoring in a bowl and mix well. Add the flour mixture, stirring just until moistened. Preheat the oven to 350 degrees. Spoon the batter into 2 buttered 5x9-inch loaf pans. Bake for 1 hour or until a wooden pick inserted in the center comes out clean. Cool in pans on a wire rack for 10 minutes. Invert onto a wire rack to cool. Serve warm or at room temperature. **Yield: 24 servings**

Applesauce Nut Bread

3 cups applesauce
1 cup unsalted butter,
   softened
1 cup milk
1/2 cup buttermilk
1/2 cup honey
3 eggs, beaten
2 teaspoons light molasses
1 1/2 cups whole wheat flour
1 cup all-purpose flour
1 cup ground oats

1/2 cup sugar
1 cup packed dark brown sugar
2 teaspoons salt
2 teaspoons cinnamon
1 1/2 teaspoons ground nutmeg
1 teaspoon baking soda
1 teaspoon baking powder
1/2 teaspoon ground cloves
1/2 teaspoon ground ginger
8 ounces pecans, chopped
2 ounces sunflower seeds

Mix applesauce, butter, milk, buttermilk, honey, eggs and molasses in a bowl. Combine whole wheat flour, all-purpose flour, oats, sugar, brown sugar, salt, cinnamon, nutmeg, baking soda, baking powder, cloves and ginger in a bowl and mix well. Add to the applesauce mixture, mixing just until moistened. Fold in pecans and sunflower seeds. Preheat oven to 350 degrees. Spoon the batter into 2 buttered 5x9-inch loaf pans. Bake for 1 hour. Cool in pans on a wire rack for 10 minutes, then remove from pans. Serve warm. **Yield: 24 servings**

Drunken Peach Cobbler

Flaky Pie Crust (page 119)
1 to 1¼ cups packed light brown sugar
2 tablespoons flour
2 tablespoons cornstarch
1 teaspoon cinnamon
½ teaspoon salt
3 pounds ripe peaches, peeled, sliced

1 cup peach schnapps
2 eggs, lightly beaten
1 teaspoon vanilla extract
¼ teaspoon almond extract
½ cup unsalted butter
1 egg
1 tablespoon heavy whipping cream
⅓ cup turbinado raw sugar

Line the bottom and sides of a 9x13-inch baking dish with some of the pie pastry. Mix 1 cup brown sugar, flour, cornstarch, cinnamon and salt in a bowl. Add peaches, tossing to coat. Increase the brown sugar by ¼ cup if the peaches are not ripe. Whisk peach schnapps, 2 eggs and flavorings in a bowl. Add to peach mixture and mix gently. Spoon the peach mixture into the prepared baking dish. Dot with butter. Preheat the oven to 400 degrees. Moisten edges of pie pastry with water. Top with remaining pastry; seal edges and flute. Mix 1 egg and whipping cream in a bowl. Brush pastry with egg mixture. Sprinkle with raw sugar. Bake for 55 minutes. **Yield: 6 to 8 servings**

Rich 'n Creamy Old-Fashioned Ice Cream

3 eggs plus 2 egg yolks
1½ cups whole milk
½ cup evaporated milk
1 cup plus 2 tablespoons sugar

¼ teaspoon salt
1 vanilla bean
2 cups heavy whipping cream
1 tablespoon vanilla extract

Beat eggs and egg yolks in a small bowl; set aside. Mix milk, evaporated milk, sugar, and salt in a heavy saucepan. Add whole vanilla bean. Cook over medium-low heat, lightly stirring frequently until milk mixture starts to simmer, about 15 minutes. Reduce heat. Add 1 cup of hot milk mixture to eggs, mixing well. Add back to milk mixture; cook for 1 minute longer. Pour into metal mixing bowl resting in ice bath. Remove vanilla pod and scrape out seeds, returning to milk mixture. Discard pod. Stir to cool, then add whipping cream and vanilla extract. Refrigerate for at least 2 hours. Place in ice cream maker and freeze according to manufacturer's directions. **Yield: 1 quart**

"May you always be surrounded by good friends and great food!"

Famous Dave

Index

Ingredient Preferences

Substitutions (only in an emergency!)

Famous Dave's Steak Seasoning:
    Morton Nature's Seasons
        Seasoning Salt
Famous Dave's BBQ Sauce:
    Your Favorite BBQ Sauce
Famous Dave's Mustard BBQ Sauce:
    Your Favorite Prepared Yellow
        Mustard

Call 1-800-210-4040 or visit our website general
store at www.famousdaves.com

Amaretto:
    Disaronno Amaretto Original
Apricot Preserves:
    Polaner All Fruit Spreadable Fruit
    Milkin Apricot Preserves
Baked Beans:
    Bush's Best Original Baked Beans
Balsamic Vinegar:
    Alessi Balsamic Vinegar
Butter Cracker Crumbs:
    Ritz Crackers
Cheddar Cheese:
    Black Diamond Cheddar
Cinnamon:
    Schilling Premium Ground
        Cinnamon
Cream Sherry:
    Harveys Bristol Cream

Dry Mustard:
    Colman's English Mustard
Flour:
    Martha White Flour
French Salad Dressing:
    The Original Western Dressing
Frozen Tangerine Juice Concentrate:
    Minute Maid Premium Tangerine
        Juice Cocktail
Hot Pepper Sauce:
    Zydeco Cayenne Pepper Sauce (best)
        distributed by Calido Chile
        Traders Systems,
        Merriam, KS 66203
    Louisiana Southern Spice
Italian Salad Dressing:
    Wish-Bone Robusto Italian
        Dressing
Italian Sausage:
    Johnsonville Italian Sausage
Key Lime Juice:
    Florribean, 155 Obispo Avenue,
    Miami, FL 33134, (800) 282-8459
Lemon Pepper:
    Schilling Lemon & Pepper
        Seasoning Salt
Mayonnaise:
    Hellmann's Real Mayonnaise
Mustard:
    Pommery French Mustard
        (Pommery Moutard de Meaux)
    Grey Poupon Country Dijon
        Mustard
    Koops' Düsseldorf Mustard

Paprika:
    Hungarian Paprika
Parmesan Cheese:
    Any good imported Italian
        Parmesan (not the dried-up
        stuff in the green can!),
        freshly grated
Peach Schnapps:
    Dekuyper Original Peachtree
        Schnapps
Pickle Relish:
    Claussen Sweet Pickle Relish
Pumpkin:
    Libby's 100% Pure Pumpkin
Salad Dressing:
    Kraft Miracle Whip
Seasoned Salt:
    Morton Nature's Seasons
        Seasoning Salt
Smoked Sausage:
    Hillshire Farm Smoked
        Sausage
Vanilla Extract:
    Sauers Vanilla Extract
    Schilling Pure Vanilla Extract
Wild Rice:
    Lake Grown & Hand Harvested
        Leech Lake Natural
        (800) 328-6731
Worcestershire Sauce:
    Lea & Perrins Worcestershire
        Sauce
Yellow Cake Mix:
    Jiffy Cake Mix

DAVID ANDERSON, the author, is a Choctaw/ Chippewa Indian as remarkably unique as his food and his award-winning restaurants. Widely recognized for his extraordinary palate, devotion to detail, and dedication to perfection, he has experienced both frustration and failure as well as tremendous success, founded three publically traded companies on Wall Street, been awarded a Bush Fellowship, received a master's degree from Harvard (without having an undergraduate degree), and been awarded "Entrepreneur of the Year Award" (in Minnesota and the Dakotas) by Ernst & Young, NASDAQ, and *USA Today*. Along the way, he has developed a wide range of interests, including music, silversmithing, and antiques, and claims his two passions in life are learning and cooking.

Today, Dave devotes himself to making a difference in his community and in the lives of others less fortunate. As an avid public speaker, he shares his optimism and inspiration with youth groups and community organizations, stressing that no matter how tough things may seem today, if you never give up your dream and work hard, tomorrow's rewards will always come. Dave lives with his wife and two sons in Edina, Minnesota.

MICHAEL W. RUTHERFORD is a national and international award-winning photographer for Fortune 500 companies, music stars, and state and national government leaders including several presidents. Photographic world travels include trips in the United States, Canada, China, Russia, Central America, and Western Europe, as well as Ireland and Scotland.

In 1997 Rutherford was commissioned by the national office of the Boy Scouts of America to photograph the first commissioned Boy Scout poster since Norman Rockwell's.

A highly regarded food photographer for over twenty years, Rutherford has had his work featured in many national and international advertising campaigns as well as in numerous cookbooks. He lives with his wife and two sons outside Nashville, Tennessee.

The photo team of Mindy, Mike, Sandra, Mary Ann, Dave, Brad, and Aubrey

Additional photography: Front end sheet and inset on page 41, courtesy of *Pittsburgh Courier* Photographic Archives, Pittsburgh, PA; Blues Club photographs courtesy of Famous Dave's BBQ Blues Club, www.famousdaves.com; Lodge photographs courtesy of Grand Pines Resort, Hayward, WI, www.grandpines.com; Pages 154–155, courtesy of Think Visuals Photography, St. Paul, MN